Dad and Dunk
in the
Great War

# Dad and Dunk
# in the
# Great War

## Jenifer Burckett-Picker

*PHP*
*Personal History Press*
*Lincoln, Massachusetts*

**Front Cover:** George W. Duncan ("Dunk") and Douglas M. Burckett ("Dad"), Nevers, France, August 1918 (JBP)

**Back Cover:** The two daughters meet—Jenifer and Margaret, Montana 2014. (JBP)

**Credits for photos and illustrations:**

| | |
|---|---|
| DY | From the collection of Duncan York |
| JBP | Taken by or in the collection of Jenifer Burckett-Picker |
| DMB | Douglas M. Burckett |
| ACE | U.S. Army Corps of Engineers, "Combat and Construction: US Army Engineers in World War I" |
| CdI | Cahiers de l'Iroise, No. 225, Brest, France |
| HM | Hoboken Museum, Hoboken, New Jersey |
| ABMC | American Battle Monuments Commission |
| LOC | U.S. Library of Congress |
| PAN | "La présence américaine dans la Nièvre", La Sermoisienne |
| CMH | U.S. Army Center of Military History |

Copyright 2018 Jenifer Burckett-Picker
ISBN-13: 978-0-9983619-4-9
Library of Congress Control Number: 2018940561

*PHP*
*Personal History Press*
*Lincoln, Massachusetts*
*www.personalhistorypress.com*

**To Dad and Dunk**

*100 years on*

*They went over
and didn't come back
till it was over
over there*

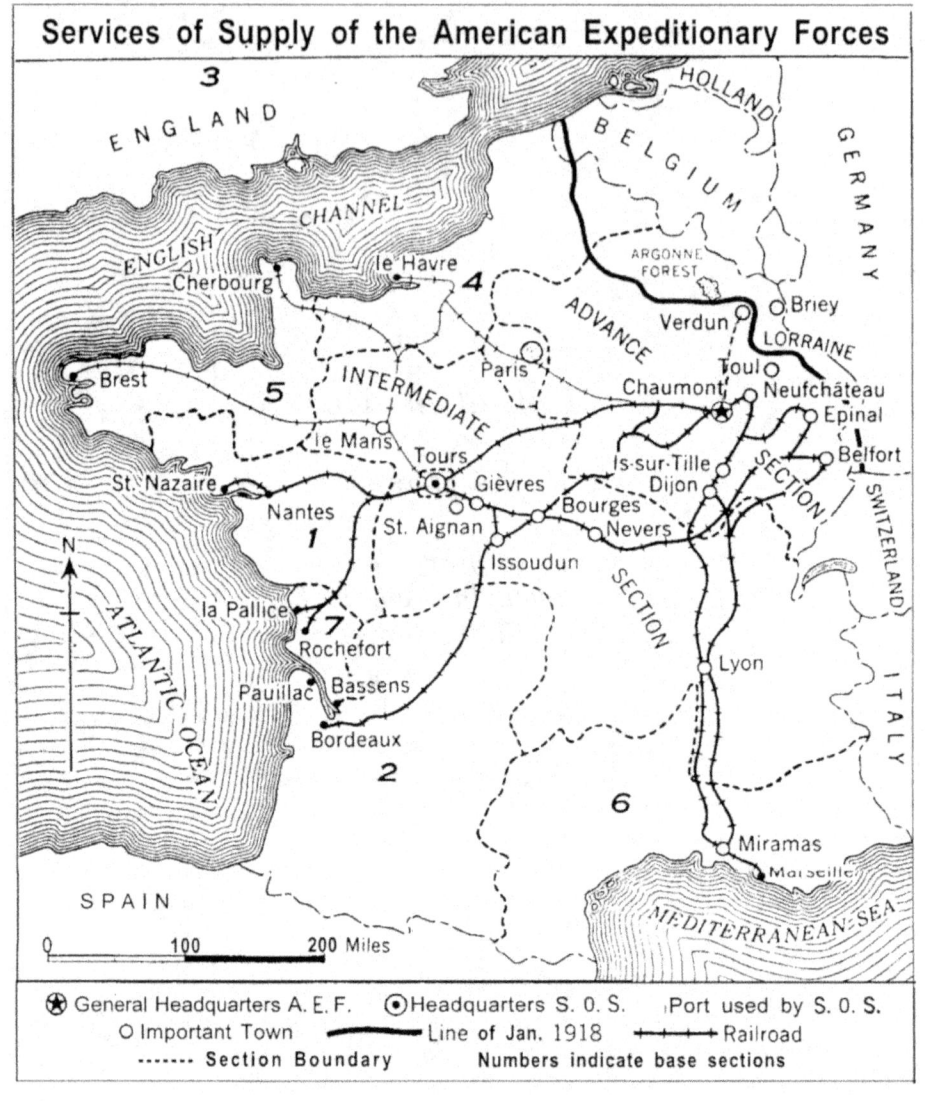

France, showing main World War I railroad routes. (ACE)

# Contents

Foreword .................................................................................... viii

Author's Preface ............................................................................ x

Chapter 1: The Trunk in the Basement ........................................... 1

Chapter 2: Dad and Dunk: East Meets West ................................... 7

Chapter 3: On the High Seas and through the Danger Zone ..... 33

Chapter 4: The Path to Pontanezen ............................................... 43

Chapter 5: La ligne américaine — the Nevers Cut-Off ................. 55

Chapter 6: Off to the Front in Verdun ........................................... 85

Chapter 7: The Return to College and Work .............................. 131

Chapter 8: The Missing Piece ....................................................... 153

Chapter 9: "Over There" a Century Later .................................. 161

Epilogue ......................................................................................... 177

Selected Bibliography .................................................................. 179

Acknowledgements ...................................................................... 184

About the Author ......................................................................... 187

# Foreword

For as long as soldiers have left home to venture into unknown parts of the globe, they have longed to return home. Jenifer Burckett-Picker captures this timeless feeling in a remarkable fashion in *Dad and Dunk in the Great War*, as she tells the story of her father, Douglas Mellen Burckett (Doug), and his good friend, George Wylie Duncan (Dunk). For this current active duty soldier reading this manuscript while deployed to Baghdad, Iraq, their words written over a hundred years ago ring just as true today. Reading through the diary entries and letters home of Doug and Dunk evoked many feelings for this soldier. The theme of constantly being homesick hit close to the mark. While reading this in Baghdad, I myself was struggling with a bout of homesickness. Doug and Dunk's message highlights a constant theme in war: no matter how many times you leave home, you always miss it and want to return.

In 1918, for men who had spent most of their lives in one place, being shipped off to various Army camps on the East Coast, experiencing a transatlantic voyage, and then living in France must have only added to that longing for home. It was with a heavy heart that I read about Dunk, older and more experienced than most soldiers, describing how he was brought to tears thinking of his girl back home.

Like Doug and Dunk, any soldier who deploys to a distant land is never sure she or he will return. Throughout history, the enemy was the least of the deploying soldier's worries: crossing a wild ocean, confronting disease, or the constant challenge of weather often proved to be greater adversaries. In the case of Doug, Dunk, and the millions of American troops who left the East Coast of the United State for Europe in World War I, those challenges were even greater. The constant threat of U-boats made any ocean crossing even more dangerous, and the horrible conditions experienced on the Western Front still echo throughout history today. Even on the modern battlefield, simple things such as field sanitation and proper hygiene are critically important to keep troops in the fight.

Too often those who have veterans in their families or family history do not hear about their experiences "over there." Whether a conscious choice or driven by something deeper, many veterans upon returning to the place they've dreamt about while gone, choose to put that previous life in the recesses of their minds, sometimes never bringing it up again. For Jenifer, finding this diary and going back to the places where her Dad and Dunk lived, worked, slept, and talked of going home, was a great way to honor their dedication to the war effort and to immortalize their selfless service to the United States.

As an active duty Army officer currently serving my fifth tour in Iraq, I relate to this narrative on a very personal level. The tone of the letters, the short but accurate diary entries, and the love shown by the writer for her "main characters" could not be more touching.

Michael D. Sullivan, Ph.D.
Colonel, United States Army
Chief's Initiative Group, Office of Security Cooperation
Baghdad, Iraq
2018

# Author's Preface

This is the story of two ordinary young soldier-engineers who enlisted for service in World War I (WWI) in the fall of 1917. One, Douglas Mellen Burckett, my dad, from New Jersey, had just finished his sophomore year at MIT in electrical engineering; the other, George Wylie Duncan, 'Dunk,' was a road engineer with the U.S. Forest Service and hailed from Missoula, Montana. This is their story as they took part in the American Expeditionary Forces, 23rd Engineers Regiment in Wagon Company #3 from 1917 to 1919, first in basic training and then on to Brest, Nevers and Verdun, France as the war raged around them.

Theirs is not a story of blood and guts, but rather a story of dedication to a war effort being waged on foreign battlefields many thousands of miles from their homes. It is the story of a friendship forged in training camps, a dangerous sea voyage, and life just behind the front lines. Their story includes construction of the most important railway project built by Americans in France during the Great War, which is completely unknown to most people now, but was vitally important in transferring American soldiers and war materiel to the Front from the Atlantic ports in 1918. It is the universally human story of yearning for home and loved ones amidst the deprivations, the mud, the rats and the all-too-common lice of the barracks, tent-cities, shelters, and dugouts in which they lived for months on end. It is a story that gives a detailed view of what life was like for these soldiers and how they reacted to being in France and surrounded by French culture. It is also a story of what it was like to return from the war and continue on with life back in the U.S. This is Dad and Dunk's story, mostly in their own voices, supplemented with insights gained by a daughter's return to World War I sites in France a century later.

The material for this book comes primarily from Dad's 1917 - 1919 diary and photos, Dunk's 1917 - 1919 letters to his girlfriend, later wife, Eileen Wagner, interviews with Dunk's daughter and grandson, and my conversations with Dad. It is supplemented by research trips that I took to Verdun in 2011 and to Brest, Nevers, and Verdun in 2017 during which I spoke to WWI historians, museum directors, French men and women passionate about WWI history, presidents of local historical societies, and daughters and sons as well as grandchildren of WWI soldiers. I have also used materials from the National Archives, the U.S. Army Corps of Engineers Publications Depot (Hyattsville, MD), and the Center of Military History of the United States Army (Washington, D.C.) regarding WWI and in particular any references to the 23rd Engineers Regiment.

NOTE: Throughout this book Dad's diary entries are in bold. Dunk's letters to Eileen are shown as block quotes in a reduced font. I have kept Dunk's original spelling.

Dad's World War I canteen and a piece of shrapnel from the Argonne found on 2017 research trip. (JBP)

# Chapter 1: The Trunk in the Basement

Children are often never old enough to care, nor wise enough to ask about their parents' pre-children lives, and I was such a child. My dad very rarely mentioned anything to do with World War I, except for some of his expressions like "up and at 'em" which for some reason I had always understood as "Up and Adam." I had no idea what it meant, except that when my dad said it to me I was usually lolling in bed on a weekend morning. I did not associate it with "over the top" from the trenches of WWI.

Dad had enjoyed singing songs like "Over There" and "Pack up Your Troubles" and "Tipperary," but I, of course, had no idea of their provenance. They seemed like catchy tunes and I was always glad to join in when we sang them around the campfire at our family summer camp or in front of a roaring blaze in the fireplace at the ski lodge we often visited in the winter.

One of Dad's prized possessions was an old aluminum canteen covered by an insulated khaki case with a metal belt attachment that he always carried on our hiking or camping trips. Many were the times that the water from this canteen slaked my sister's and my thirst as we followed our parents up mountain trails from an early age. This WWI general army-issue canteen now sits on my desk urging me to continue writing this book.

Dad had sometimes spoken about George Duncan, "Dunk," his best buddy from those long ago days when they met at a training camp in Maryland before they shipped over to France on the same transport. They spent over a year together, 1918 - 1919, enduring some dismal conditions as they worked just behind the front lines building and repairing roads, railroads and bridges, and helping construct the all-important railway cut-off south of Nevers that enabled the Americans more efficiently to send soldiers and materials from the Atlantic ports to the Front. Dad had spoken adoringly of Dunk's girlfriend and later wife, Eileen. In fact, as some of Dunk's letters to Eileen show, my dad had encouraged Dunk to write to his girlfriend more often.

After the war and after Dad graduated from MIT, he was looking for an adventure, but also a job. Dunk, who was working for the United States Forest Service (USFS) out of Missoula, Montana had encouraged Dad to come west to get a job using his engineering skills with the USFS to help survey and open up the road network necessary to enlarge the timber industry operations in western Montana and in Idaho. So Dad hitchhiked to Missoula in 1922, joined up with Dunk, and got a job with the USFS as a surveyor and truck driver.

A few years later, in 1924, Dunk and Eileen's daughter Margaret was born. She led a rather peripatetic life as a child, because both of her parents were then working for the USFS— Dunk as a road engineer and Eileen as an accountant. The young family was often housed in USFS camps or in very small towns, as the virgin forests were being opened up to the mammoth logging operations to support the increasing demand for timber. Dad had, therefore, met Margaret as a small child, and when he spoke about her in later years, it was always with great affection.

On a family trip west in 1960 we drove to the Lake Coeur d'Alene area of eastern Idaho so that Dad could return to the places he had worked as a young man forty years before with the USFS. As a teenager, all I can remember is the endless miles of bumpy dirt roads that we traversed, dying of the heat and eating dust with not a soul in sight. I must have loudly protested, so that eventually we got to stop by a cool stream and go swimming, hanging our clothes on the tree limbs.

On this same trip, and perhaps even the same day, we drove to Missoula and stopped by a house so my dad could visit his old friend Eileen, Dunk's wife. Dunk had died of a burst appendix, due to poor medical care, in 1945, and Eileen had eventually remarried a Mr. Anderson. They continued to live in Missoula, in the home Eileen and Dunk had bought three decades earlier. I was the ever-rebellious teen and refused to leave the car to visit Dad's old friend. I remember sitting

Douglas M. Burckett, 91 year-old WWI veteran, marches in Lincoln, Massachusetts, 4th of July parade on July 4, 1987. (JBP)

in the car in front of the house hoping that the visit would soon be over. It turned out that daughter Margaret was then married and living with her husband and children in eastern Washington. Our paths, therefore, did not cross in 1960.

Dad was proud of his service in World War I and he got to show this annually in our town's Fourth of July parade. He always marched at the front with the veterans in his uniform, except the year he was grand marshal and rode in a convertible. His canteen was hooked to his belt on one side and the revolver was on the other. His army-issue khaki shirt and hat were complemented by a pair of regular khaki work pants. Being an anti-war child of the 1960s, this was not something that I really thought my dad should be doing. Other townspeople were very impressed, however, that Dad had kept his trim figure from over a half century before and was still able to fit into his twenty-something uniform. They were also impressed that well into his nineties he was able to walk the mile-long parade route, keeping up with men half his age.

There was a small trunk in our house that my husband kept telling me to clean out as it was "cluttering the basement area" that he wanted to use for his hobbies. My dad had died at age ninety-seven in 1993 and when, after almost a decade, I finally got around to opening this trunk, I found it was a treasure trove of my dad's World War I memorabilia. In it were the revolver (containing no bullets), victory medals attesting to my dad's participation in both the St. Mihiel and Meuse-Argonne Offensives, old maps of the Western Front in the area of Verdun, the khaki army hat and shirt, Dad's Army discharge papers, and a small, partially disintegrated, brittle envelope with something inside.

I had a feeling that the envelope contained something important. And it did! Inside was a packet of 2.5 inch by 4.5 inch white lined pages with three holes punched at the top. Written mostly in ink but occasionally in pencil was Dad's diary from November 25, 1917, when he was sworn into service at Ft. Slocum, New York to June 14, 1922 when he left Boston on route to western Montana. In these miniature pages, in a tiny but very readable script, was my dad's record of his World War I service.

As I began to read these pages, I was filled with emotion. They told story of my dad's time in the service, and what captivated me was the friendship he had formed with one of the soldiers he'd met in training camp. George "Dunk" Duncan was from rural Montana and Dad, who had interrupted his studies at MIT to join the war, was from New Jersey. They became fast friends as they spent months in training camps in Maryland and then went overseas together. As I read through the diary I knew I wanted to dig deeper into this decades-long relationship.

Pages from Dad's 1917-1919 diary. (DMB)

Camp Meade, Maryland, in World War I. Over 400,000 soldiers passed through here during the war. (CMH)

# Chapter 2: Dad and Dunk: East Meets West

How did a Forest Service employee from western Montana with a partial high school education become such good friends with an electrical engineering student from the Massachusetts Institute of Technology? What drew them to each other and how did their relationship continue for many decades after the war was over? How is it that their descendants, a hundred years later, still continue that friendship?

It all started at Camp Meade, Maryland at the end of December 1917. This camp had opened in July 1917 as a training camp for soldiers, particularly engineers. Dad had been there since the first of the month when Dunk arrived on a cold late December day. Dad was "sworn into service," as he says in his diary, on November 25, 1917 at Fort Slocum, New York—a major recruiting station for New England, New York, and New Jersey. Dunk had enlisted in Missoula, Montana, and after going to Spokane, Washington for induction, had been sent east on a five-day train journey to Camp Meade, arriving there on December 23rd. Both Dunk and Dad were assigned to Wagon Company #3 of the 23rd Engineers. There were only about 150 men in the company, so it was not hard to meet the others.

But what would have attracted Dad and Dunk to each other? What would each of them have seen in the other that would have made them strike up a conversation? Trying to put the pieces together a hundred years later is challenging, but some characteristics of each of them stand out.

Dad and Dunk were both natural leaders. They were competent individuals who were not afraid to take charge when necessary. Dad had just turned twenty-two on December 18th and Dunk was about to turn thirty on January 26th. Both had lost their mothers at an early age and had fathers who were emotionally distant, unable to connect with their sons on a personal level. Dad had lost his beloved older brother when he was ten and then lost his sister, in a car accident, while he was in France. Dunk had two younger sisters, but both were estranged from the family due to their choices of husbands. So in many ways their personal lives were similar. Perhaps Dad saw in Dunk the older brother that he had so admired, and Dunk recognized in Dad the younger brother that he had never had.

Both were engineers, interested in similar disciplines. Dad was an electrical engineering student who had finished his second year at MIT. Dunk had been working for over a decade as a "road engineer" for the U.S. Forest Service out of their western Montana field office in Missoula. He helped survey and build roads to open up the huge tracts of forest there which were being exploited by the timber industry. He also worked on cars and trucks. Both were mechanically oriented and enjoyed understanding how things worked and how things could be built.

Family backgrounds, undoubtedly, also played a part in Dad and Dunk's enduring friendship. Both of their mothers had been born in Glasgow, Scotland. In fact Dunk's parents had emigrated from Scotland to Montana and Dunk had been born in North Dakota in 1888 on route to Missoula. Dad's mother retained close ties with her family in Scotland by taking Dad there on two visits before she died. Both Dad and Dunk came from families of hard-working Protestant immigrants. They had these certain common values with which they had both been raised.

But why did both of them enlist in the Army to go fight in a country that neither of them knew, on another continent many thousands of miles away from home? Was this out of a sense of duty, for patriotism, in a quest for adventure, or were there other factors involved? Had their fathers encouraged them to do so, or their friends, or in the case of Dad his classmates at MIT?

Like many other questions that come up a century later, we will never know what their exact motivations were for enlisting. We can only surmise that a sense of patriotism and/or a yearning for adventure was what prompted them both to sign up. The war in Europe had been going on since August

1914 with the major Allied nations of Great Britain, France, and Russia fighting against the major Central Powers of Germany and the Austro-Hungarian Empire. Although the U.S. remained somewhat neutral it had been sending many more merchant vessels to trade with the Allies than with the Central Powers. In fact, as German submarines (U-boats) patrolled the Atlantic to sink enemy ships, there were several American merchant ships which had been attacked. Passenger ships carrying Americans, most notably the *Lusitania* in 1915, had also been attacked and sunk by U-boats. So although the U.S. was not officially in the war, ships with Americans aboard were being preyed upon by the Germans.

In early 1917 due to another series of diplomatic events, President Woodrow Wilson, who had been reelected on a promise of non-intervention, was finally persuaded to ask Congress to declare war on Germany. Congress approved the declaration on April 6, 1917 and the U.S. formally entered the war on the side of the Allies.

Dunk's first letter to his girlfriend Eileen from Camp Meade, Maryland was written on December 23, 1917, the day he arrived there. It gives us a vivid picture of how things were at these camps that had been hastily assembled by the Army to train the millions of soldiers needed for the war effort that General Pershing had promised the Allies. Dunk wrote:

> Got in 3:00 o'clock this morning had 1 hr. sleep having a great time (?) 35,000 men here 13,000 horses, 12 square miles of grounds, every body very busy rather could, I'll write you a good letter as soon as I have a chance. I'm writing this on the fly. Just got inoculated again, may be knocked out for a day or so so don't be alarmed if you don't hear from me. I would have wished you Marry Christmas but can't get away

For Dad and Dunk life in the training camps was quite regimented. Men were up early, had to work or train all day, and then had "lights out" at 10:00 p.m. They were exhausted by then, as Dunk mentions in many of his letters to Eileen. This exhaustion combined with the huge numbers of men sharing one large room or a large tent made any attempt to get away and write a personal letter to a loved one very difficult. Dunk also writes to Eileen that each soldier was only issued three sheets of paper and an envelope per day, and that most of this was used for his letters to her.

Crowded army camp life includes the lack of sleep due to the constant coughing at night of the 175 men sharing a room at Camp Meade, as Dunk notes in one of his letters. Also, the men were receiving constant inoculations and had to be quarantined, sometimes for weeks at a time. Some of them became sick, either due to the inoculations or the constant cold which they had to bear in the midst of a Maryland winter, often without proper clothing. The Army was not yet ready in early 1918 to outfit all of the recruits with uniforms and warm winter boots, hats, sweaters, and socks. The winter of 1917-1918 went on record as the coldest winter in the last century. The average January temperature was twenty-four degrees Fahrenheit, but often dipped into the single digits and even at times to below zero. This was brutally bitter for those on guard duty without proper winter clothing.

All of these issues are noted by Dunk in his January 9th to 11th, 1918, letters to Eileen from Camp Meade, in which he notes that he still has not received clothes from the O.D. (Office of Defense). He describes his twelve-hour overnight guard duty in the bitter cold and how very thankful he is for the muffler and "scarfe" that Eileen and her sister Irma knit for him. He mentions in several letters how much her letters cheer him up ("the sun came out today…"). His letters express emotion and homesickness for the people and places he's left behind— universal feelings of so many of the young soldiers who were away from home for the first time. The "C.W.C.s" that he references in many of his letters were friends with whom he and Eileen used to socialize and play cards. The letters also express deep thanks to those who care enough to write to him and send him food and clothing.

At this time Eileen was a student at the University of Montana in Missoula, and Dunk often expressed his hope

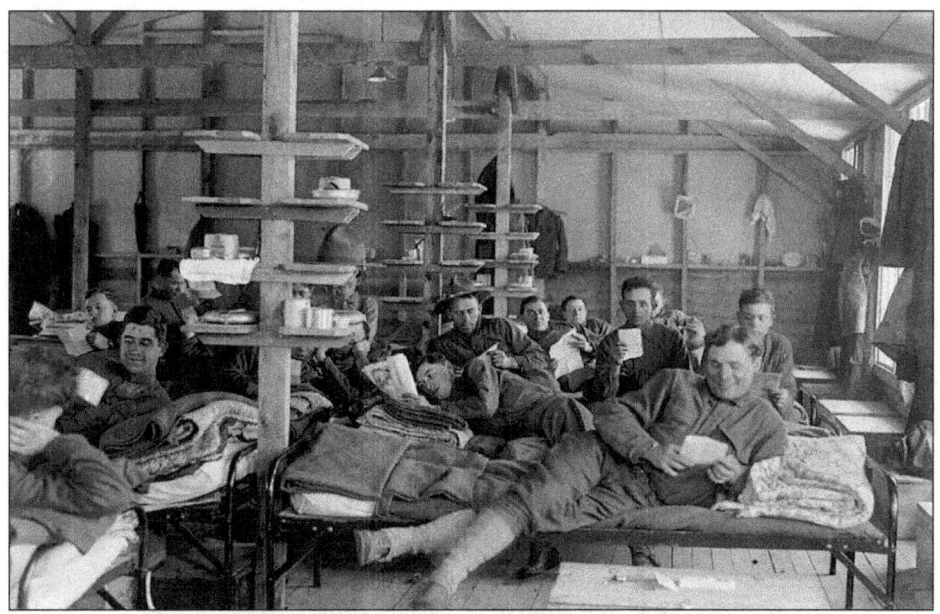

Relaxing in barracks at Camp Meade, Maryland, World War I. (CMH)

that she was doing well in her studies. Irma, Eileen's sister mentioned in the January 10th letter, was tall and blond and needed a boyfriend, so Dunk decided to match her up with one of his army mates, who was also tall and needed a girlfriend. Notes about this continuing "romance" appear in several of Dunk's subsequent letters.

Dunk is able to express himself very tenderly and often mentions how Eileen and her mother (whom Dunk refers to as "Mother") are the only family he has that cares about him. As previously noted, Dunk's mother had died many years earlier, his father was emotionally distant, and his sisters were estranged from the family. This made Dunk appreciate all the more the love and caring that he received from Eileen's family.

C.M. Md.

1/9/18

Dearest Girl:-

Well the sun came out to-day, when the mail came in, because I got a letter from you dear, and it was'nt half so hard to drill as it has been in fact I liked to drill quite a lot better. I just posted you a letter to-day but what difference does it make, if you think they are coming a little to thick why you can let this one go for a day or so before you read it.

Dear, you mustn't amagin any thing when you don't hear from me because I'm just as safe as a needle in a hay stack and I'd be just about as easy for a stranger to fine here, in a way they take mighty good care of us that is if we don't get sick, and that is left pretty much up to us, we're not supposed to get sick. To-day is the first day since I landed here that I've felt half way myself but I think now I'm going to be all right, of course every one has a bad cough but mine is getting pretty good now, I don't cough at all at night and I think by the time you receive this I'll be all right, you ought to see this place though there is about 175 men in this one room and it sounds like a den of sea lions. First one barks then an other and then they all bark.

Eileen dear I'm afraid your getting desperate when you start taking that stuff on board, I only wish I'd been there to, and I'd have been as sick as you were I'd do any thing, but there is'nt a chance to do any thing here you can't even sit up later than 10:00 o'clock and I don't think, any one is cares much about that any more.

Talk about clever girl are'nt you the good one though, poor little kid I'll bet you needed the extra sleep though when you did get the chance, I don't blame you for sleeping in, after that seage.

I have'nt received the pkg. yet dear but I expect it will come along soon now, do you know they have'nt even been able to give me a shirt yet and your swetter is acting shirt and swetter to now, its' a little low necked so the muffler sure will be most greatfully received, I wore the swetter backwords so the V is in the back and in that way it comes up pretty good.

The ristlets are sure going to be a fine thing to, I never suffered so with cold hands and rist before, I don't savie this climate at all, its' kind of damp and so cold that the ice never thaws at all, so the cold just cuts right through you, and to make it real nice the blame wind always blows just enough to push the cold in.

Did you ever get chil blanes on your ears? Well I got 'em my ears have frozen and thawed so often I don't pay any attention to them any more. I feel guilty letting you do so much for me though when I can do seemingly nothing for you.

If every body comes as near doing their 'bit' as you do for to make me comfortable, the war wont last long or then we're not much good, and from the look of the boys here and what they are putting up with, with a smile I think we won't take long if ever we get to the front, I've did a good deal of kicking to you and I'm ashamed of it but right here we don't kick, we just go to it and do what we can to make our company show up, and so far we have showed up pretty good, even with the cold weather and ice which are not at all good to drill with.

I won't say we don't kick on any thing either we do kick some on the grub, all of us because that can be helped and I guess will in time.

Well Darling take care of your self and don't go to strong on the champagne I heard that its' after effects are hard on the system, especially the morning after.

Tell me about your studies dear did I make you loose your whole half year?

That really worries me a lot because its something that can't be made up.

I'm not a quitter but if this thing was over to-morrow and they'd say I could go home I'd start right out walking that's just how bad I'd like to get back , and 420 Blane St. would be the first place I'd stop.

Dear you need not be afraid of any censorship here, they wont censor any thing tell we go across and I've got my doubts if we'll ever get across.

It's getting cold in here so I guess Id better cut this and turn in Regard to every body, and just remind C.W.C's they owe me a letter right away.

Jan 10 1918

Just received your letter sweetheart and you have no idea how very very glad I was to get it, that makes three I've received, and every time one comes the sun comes out.

I'm more pleased over your getting by this exam I think than any thing else though, I felt mighty guilty about that.

You poor little orphan you, I wish I was there to look after you, I'd light the fires, and carry in the wood and also; keep you up late nights.

I haven't received the box yet dear but I suppose its' like every think else it will come in time, but time seems to be a mighty indefinite thing here.

Gee! I wish I could have been there for that crab dinner, but I guess we have more crabs for dinner than any one else only we don't eat'em.

Tell Irma I got that soldier for her all right, and if she'll guarantee to feed him and take care of him I'll send him along he's 6 ft. 4 in. and waighs 195#, has a southern drall, is dark complected, has an appetite for candy and cake, and is particularly partial to blond girls, the only way she can get any mail to him though will be through me all of which I hold the right to censor especialy the candy and cakes.

Why dear we're quarentined for every thing on the out side of a patent medicine bottle, how ever I'm just feeling fine and I don't think I could catch any thing now if I tried.

You bet I know I've been gone a month honey and three days more and it seems like I'd been gone two years I never was in a place where time passed so slowly as it does here.

Dearest I'm going to try to fix it so you won't have to watch the postman to no avail any more, I'm not sure I can do this but I'm going to try to.

I'm mighty sorry your Christmas holidays were such a fizzle, when we might have had a dandy time if I'd not been a fool and enlisted in this darned army.

I'm mighty glad you have the Wilken's so handy that sure helps a lot, how are Calkins and the neighbor making it?

Honey you have did a lot too many things for me now, I have a feeling that I have imposed on you. You have did so much, I have a family or I had one once that should look after me but they don't even take the time to write and answer my letter, if it was'nt that they may have some mail of mine there that I want I'd never write them an other line, but I mustn't worry you with that.

I guess I'd better close this and get it in the mail or you wont get it for a week.

Be good to your self sweetheart and if you can find the time to write to me occasionally you will be doing all I can ask,

    Yours in arms darling

        Dunk. (my official tital)


                        Camp Meade, Md. 1/11/18

Dearest Girl:-

The package came to-day and I can't thank you enough for it gee but it was good, I was on guard duty when it came and one of the boys that was in the baricks sick got it for me and came out and told me it was there twenty minutes before I got off. Say that was the longest 20 minutes I ever spent and if I had knowen how good it was, I'm sure it would have been twice as long.

I was awful cold and and hungry when I came in and I ate about half of it without stopping and a fellow sleeping next to me is sick and got the gripe I think and I gave him some and he said it was the first thing he'd eaten for two days, so I went and got him a cup of coffee and gave him some more and he's going to pray for you he says, he's a pretty nice kid a nephew of General Bell commander of the forces at Staten Island New York.

I have been borrowing a scarfe when I went on guard lately, you know I never thought much about this guard duty and I didn't think how cold a job it was till I got some and take it from me you can't get clothes enough to keep you warm, try it some time when its real cold at night, it'll do you a lot of good, I don't think. I went on last night at nine thirty stood till 11:30 slept till 3:30 stood till 5:30 slept till 7:00 went on at 9:30 stood till 11:00 and I've still got an other shift its' been twenty four hours since I had my shoes of, this is what they call training I guess we'll be soldiers all right by the time we get through. I'm not kicking I'm just telling you so you will be able to realize how nice that swetter and scarfe is, I can't tell you any other way my vocabulary is too limited.

When I got here I had to go out for signal practice so I could'nt finish, I've just finished supper now had beans a boiled spud a cup of soupe and a slice of bread no meat to-day. But I had a good big peace of your cake so feel very well satisfied. That cake is sure the best I ever taisted I want to say.

This is saving paper is'nt dear well it's not so very easy to get here so it's up to us to hang on to it. They issue us three sheets and an envelope every day and if I'm not mistaken you get most of 'em, and theres no one that deserves them more than you do.

I just received a letter from C.W.C.'s to-night, and you don't know how good it seems to get it and know the folks back home are thinking about you.

Dearest I must write Irma a note on the back of this now and then go and take a bath and wash my towl to-morrow is inspection and we must have a clean towl if nothing else. So I'll say good night, to you dear little girl.

Yours always Dunk

On the back of the second page of this letter and continuing on to a third page is a letter to Irma, Eileen's sister, dated also Jan 11, 1918.

Dear Irma:-

I owe you a regular fat long letter for what you have did for me, but we don't have any more time here than the law allows the lights go out at 10:00 and most of the time we have some orders to memorize or code to practice or guard duty to stand. I just got of a 24 hour shift take it from me those are the times when mufflers came handy, but so far they haven't given me any O.D. shirt yet, so Eileens sweater is woren clear around the clock and now your muffler will catch it because the sweater neck is low the way it should be and my throat is soar all the time so now I expect to get well right away I want to tell you you never did a more appreciated thing in your life than to make me that. I was realy suffering for it honest I was, I borrowed some one elses when I could but most of the time they needed their own so I had to go with out.

I saw Dick Johnson to-day for a few minutes while I was on guard your not supposed to talk on guard but we took a chance any way, and Mrs Tucker just sent him a swetter and he says it sure saved his life he's in a truck co. and drives a big Mack. He had on an O.D. shirt a blue flannel and a sweater. Oh! Its' sure cold her.

Eileen seems to give you most of the credit for the cake, you have no idea how good it keept till it got here but it's not keeping very will now, between Ge. Bells nephew and I we've almost finished 2/3 of it. Things are sure mighty busy around here, moving troops, back and forth but so far I don't see any move in sight for me, but we have to get out of here before the next draft as this is a draft camp, however any move we make will just be a short move, and we'll be stationed in this country, till late spring I'm pretty sure, though every body here is crazy to go across, and I'm fool enough to feel the same way about it. I'd hate like the duce to get turned down now, but there is still one more chance, and this last exam is getting a lot of 'em.

Well I guess its' time for me to be getting along so I'll say good-night and hike along.

As Ever<br>George

Camp Meade, Maryland, where Dad and Dunk met and spent their first month or so together, was a "draft camp." This meant that it was an initial training camp for those men who had either enlisted or been drafted into the Army. The U.S. Selective Service Act, to insure that there were enough men in the military, had been signed into law on May 18, 1917. Men between the ages of twenty-one and thirty were required to register for the draft. During WWI over 20 million men registered and 2.8 million of them were drafted. Both Dad and Dunk had enlisted, but in the early stages of America's entry into the war both enlistees and draftees were often quartered in the same training camps.

Dunk's letter above of January 11, 1918 indicates that he and Dad would be moving to another camp soon, because Camp Meade would be used to welcome the next wave of entering soldiers. Dunk also notes that he doesn't think he'll be going "across" to France anytime soon, probably not until late spring, but mentions how both he and most of his fellow soldiers are eager to get to France. All soldiers had to pass physical exams before they were approved for final deployment, and Dunk just hopes that he won't "get turned down."

A few days later during his last week at Camp Meade, Dunk was feeling very blue and wrote one of the most heart-wrenching letters to Eileen, in which he confides to her his innermost feelings. He admits to her that he sometimes cries himself to sleep, something quite difficult for a strong man of thirty to confess, I imagine. He also tells her how he wished they'd gotten married before he enlisted. He worries that as a single man all his assets (some $15,000 worth, which was no small sum in 1918) would go to his family, which doesn't care about him. He would prefer that it go to Eileen and hopes that he can figure out some way to make that happen. Then he tries to assure her that nothing will ever happen to him, so that she shouldn't worry. Dunk also mentions that he finally received a letter from someone in his immediate family—his sister Hope.

It is in this letter, too, that he says that he thought he'd been appointed construction foreman of Wagon Company #3, but that it seems to have fallen through. He notes that there seems to be a lot of activity at Camp Meade to get the first battalion ready to go to France and the rest of the soldiers are feeling the lack of attention. Dad, however, as mentioned in his diary, was assigned to Wagon Company #3, 23rd Engineers, on January 8, 1918, just the week before. Dunk, a few days after writing the January 13th letter, was also formally assigned to Wagon Company #3.

And so Dunk pours his heart out to Eileen …

Jan 13, 1918

Dear Little Girl:-

I have'nt any thing to tell you to night but so you wont have to watch that post man in vain about the end of the week I'm going to write any way, to-nights poker night is'nt it? I wonder if your over to Cheathams to-night – playing New Market and dealing me a hand once in a while? I hope so, yes I'm mean enough to even hope your feeling as lonesome for me as I am for you, if you are your feeling mighty blue and, the lights look pretty dim. Up at the other end of the baricks some one is playing "So Long Letty," and it just seems to take the heart right out of me and send it home to you, I can see you on that piano bench as plane as if I was there, and Irma behind you singing and mother sitting rocking in the arch way, Gee! I can't think about you that way or I'll go crazy here, I have to fight myself all the time to keep from going bugs, some times when I go to bed and the lights go out I lay awake for hours looking back into that home that was so good to me, and its' mighty hard to make me cry but a time or two, I've felt something run down my cheeks that felt mighty like they might be tears, and I guess they were.

I had a letter from Hope, and one from C.W.C. and Mrs C.W.C. last week that sure was mighty good to get. Hope says my dad has gone to Cal. but she didn't say why or any thing about him, and he has never taken the trouble to write to me, and I don't suppose he will, I don't believe I ever got a letter from him in my life.

I wish now I was married, to be frank about it, I don't know who'ed want me, but I get so sore at my family I wish I had some one else to look to for thing and to do things for, I never thot much about it before but here I am with about $15,000.00 counting insuraence and every thing else and if I had a wife I could send her $30.00 a month besides and as it is I've got to leave the whole thing to a family that would'nt turn a hand for me. That is if I can't fix it so I can leave some of it for you which I sure hope I can, I'd like to feel some one was getting it that cared for me, if any thing happens to me. How ever I don't suppose any things will happen so whats the worry, but some way I get blue on that subject about ever so often.

You'd be surprised how many of the fellows are married here, I supposed there would'nt be a man in here married but every once in a while some fellow breaks loose telling about his wife, and believe me they'es the homesickest bunch you ever saw, but they all live here in the east and can get away before they go over, to go home for a few days, and that's all they talk about, I think they get 2 weeks off.

Well dear this is getting to be quite a long letter isn't it, I didn't suppose I'd go this far when I first started, but now I've got rid of my pet peeve, I guess I'd better quite.

Honey I expect your powerful busy, but any time you can you'll drope me a line wont you, I'm not as busy right now as I will be pretty soon and I've written oftener than I expect I'll be able to later, I understand we are to move into tents in a few days up at a place called Laural, so when we get there I suppose things will be bum I won't feel like writing but I'll sure try to, no matter how bum they get.

I thot by now I'd be assigned to a Co but they have been so busy getting the first batellion ready to send across they've forgotten all about the rest of us, I thot for a while I was signed up with Wagon Co #3 as construction foreman but that seems to have fallen through now, how ever it may only be asleep, according to the dope now I wont get away before spring unless I'm put into an other Co. from the Wagon Co.

Well dear I guess I'd better ring off and give you a rest. I wish we had studied some French to-gether now, we are having French classes here, how ever I'm not taking any on yet.

Best regards to the Family, and C.W.C's when you see them.

Always yours

Geo.

Dunk cheered up when he received his next letter from Eileen, which included her photo. Dad and Dunk had to endure some fairly nasty conditions during the winter of early 1918 at their various training camps in Maryland, but it is with a wonderful sense of humor in this letter that Dunk describes the dishwashing process at camp as well as the "ice rain" that keeps falling. He also encloses a page of cartoons from the *Philadelphia Evening Bulletin* which have to do with the war, Army, and conditions in camps, to which he has written a retort by each cartoon. He refers to them by saying, "The following will explain the life here just to a te."

Camp Meade. Md.

Jan. 17, 1918

Dearest Girl:-

Last night the stares came out brighter and my straw tick was softer and my breakfast taisted better this morning, and the drills on the icey field were'nt so hard, all because I got a letter from you, and the picture, Gee! Is'nt that a peach of a picture, you don't know how very very glad I was to get it. There is one thing though that puzzles me I never did get that first one you said you sent in my first letter you wrote.

...

The worst yet is the dish washing which amounts to this they set out two tubs about half full of hot water, and then we pass in at one side of the mess room eat and out the other side washing our dishes as we go, in these mess lines there is generally about 250 men, you can amagin what those tubs are like by the time the last man gets to them, they are thick as a rule, and the water is cold, and you got to use it or nothing, I've got a towl how ever I use to wash mine with, and when it gets too dirty I put it through a prossess of of hot water and soap, that is some astonishing, I want to say.

...

Poor dear your sure having your share of weather to are'nt you I thot that fine weather couldn't last very much longer, at this time of the year. This is the queerest country we have ice rains every few days and when they come the grounds is covered with about half an inch of solid ice which will stay on for two or three days and then it gets a little warm and goes off and then along comes an other rain.

...

I'm inclosing a peace of self explanitory evidence, every bit of it is so true to live it bring me to tears, save it, it will be worth a million in 10 years.

Well Dearest this is some news paper isn't it comic supliment and all, is'nt it and I think its about enough for this time. I'll close and turn in its about 10.00 P.M.

Most anciously waiting for an other letter.

Yours Always

George

From Camp Meade, where Dad and Dunk were until January 19, 1918, they moved together to Camp Glen Burnie, also in Maryland, for further Army training. Already at Camp Glen Burnie Dad had a photo of Dunk in his diary labelled

> **George W. Duncan 'Desert Rat' Wagon Co. #3, 23rd Eng. Taken at Camp Glen Burnie, Md. Feb. 1918. 'Dunk' hails from Missoula, Mont. Made a Cpl. @ Camp Laurel; promoted to Sgt. Old Mill Nevers, France; May. 1918. Apt'd Wgn. Master about Oct. 15, 1918 at Camp Mud Hole near Esnes. Married Miss Eileen Wagner Sept 22nd 1920 at Missoula, Mont. Margaret Eileen born 3/3/24. Died Feb. 19th 1945 Ruptured appendix**

Note that Dad added several of these notations to the diary after the war.

The photo of Dunk shows him in civilian clothes—a dark long-sleeved shirt rolled up to the elbows and dark pants—in

Dunk at Camp Glen Burnie, Maryland (DMB)

front of a large white canvas tent held up by posts which appear to be whole trees with the bark still on them. He seems to be walking somewhere with his arms out in front of him with a peaceful look on his face.

So what was life like at Camp Glen Burnie for Dad and Dunk? It was a hastily constructed tent camp with 230 tents with some nine or ten men per small tent. The camp was an overflow facility for soldiers from Camp Meade and only in use from 1917-1918. While at Camp Meade, although winter conditions were brutally cold and icy, at least they had lived in wooden barracks. At Glen Burnie, with even more intense cold and several feet of snow at times, Dad and Dunk were living in tents.

Dunk describes the conditions in this tent city in his January 22nd and January 25th letters to Eileen. They are still in quarantine—this time for mumps.

> Camp Glen Burnie, Md.
> Jan. 22, 1918
>
> Eileen Dear:-
>
> Your letter came last night little girl and I'll start to answer it now but what luck I'll have I don't know, it snowed 6 in. here last nigh and its' still snowing like the duce but we're right out in it building camp as fast as we can, but I'm feeling pretty good so it does'nt make any difference. Right now we're waiting for dinner, the woods all green here and the cook can't get the fire to go so its' late. I sure have a duce of a time to write here, theres 10 of us here in one small tent and we don't get only half a candle at a day so we don't have any time to write at night a-tall, we sit around in the dark till bed time and then light our candle and make our beds and save what has'nt burned up to get up by in the morning so please don't be too discouraged Dear if you don't hear as often as you expect to, because I'm writing as often as I can, though you may not think it. Right here they tooted the horn and I flew for chow.
>
> Well Dear the only way I can account for you not having gotten a couple more letters is that they have'nt reached you yet, but I'm sure you have 'em now so why worry. Oh! Yes I'm still in quarantine and expect to be for some time yet but if we're lucky now we may get out in a week or so, when we moved down here we thot we'd get out but they slapped us right back in.
>
> Poor dear little girl I'm awful sorry school is so hard, and disiagreable, you better chuk it and come East and see me for a change, very possible thing is'nt it?
>
> Yes, and if I'd get a letter from her I surely would feel highly honered and whats more I'm just egotistic enough to believe she will write me the seventh letter. Gee honey I'm awful glad you passed every thing I think that

worried me more than any thing else.

Well honey I'm glad you can feel that way about the war business, and I think your about right, I don't have any idea we'll go over either, I'm beginning to think we may be put on work right in this country.

You ought to hear this bunch, you would'nt think they were worring about this war business any, when they give us enough to eat we're the most care free bunch on earth.

Honey I hardly understand, can it be that you are getting tired writing or what is it? If you had'nt been so good to me, I'd think by your letter you were tired of it, but I don't think your that sort by a long shot, cheer up dear, and forget the worries I'm going to quite worring, and talking about my pet peaves I have'nt got any worries any more.

No dear the magazines have'nt come yet but they'll get here all right in time, it seems we're not to get any mail except once a week here now, so you see it's libe to be some time before I even get a letter.

Tell all the folks hello! For me and go down and take in a picture show for me, and dance a dance for me and, have a good Sunday dinner for me, and you'll be doing me a great good because those are the most remote thing in life to me these days. If ever I get out of quarantine I'm going up to Baltimore or Wash. D.C and have a square meal and go to a picture show, and be a regular D__ I sure wish you could be along, because its' going to be some celibration, I'll have to buy my self a pair of shoes though and a hat, or I'll be run in.

Well dear its' getting dark so I must close, you see I'm writing this in instalments.

Good night and cheer up.

Yours

    Geo

Best regards to mother and Irma.

Address me Glen Burnie MD.

    Wagon Co #3

    23rd Eng.

Camp Glen Burnie, Md
Jan. 25, 1918

Eileen Dear !!

What a clever girl I have got. I received the box and your two dandy letters to-night, and then I opened up this tablet to write and there was an-other letter, why dear I'm just tickled to death of course I'm not quite dead but, a million thank yous would'nt half express my appreciation.

Is'nt this pen a dandy thot, it sure makes writing a lot easer. I think I'll have to write every day from now on wheather I can or not. I always feel like writing every night but the chances are mighty poor we get one candle each night now or I should say ½ half a candle each nigh, and there is nine of us in this tent, so we take turns writing, just as many get around the candle as possible and write each night and the rest tell storys or swap lies about what they were before they joined the army, and believe me its' sure hard to consentrate on a letter and say what you want to in all the racket, and we can't have any light after 10:00 bells, so you see how it is, day times we work or answer roll calls, we have a tent city here now 230 tents. And it sure makes quite a sight.

Darling I could go through the box and thank you for each thing indivudaly but I guess you know how much they are appreciated the apples brought me back to C.W.C.'s and those good old poker days, the candy means you and the piano and the cake, Mother dearer to me than any one else except you. The magazine of course brings thots of C.W.C.s when we just used to go in and sit down, and read and smoke good cigeretts and be comfortable, and those cigeretts brought back, every thing to-gether and gave it all a flavor of home. I'll see that the ristlets are placed where they will be appreciated as they should be. Gen. Bell's nephew and I were put in to different Co.s so we only see each other once in a while, I would see him oftener but I'm still in quarantine, so I can't go around any, how ever he looked me up a couple of times and brook in on my quarantine.

> The ristlets and helmet came last night, and dear they'er the very best I've seen, you sure are a great little nitter, why the helmet was just exactly as it should have been, it just fit right, and sure is nice and warm. I can get a hair cut now, with out catching cold as if I could catch any more.
>
> We're quarantined now for mumps can you beat it they took one of the boys out of our tent to the base hospital this morning with 'em. I've had 'em so I don't have to worry.
>
> Darling girl I must close now my candle is just about in, and I must have enough to get to bed by, I'd like to write on for an hour but no chance, so Good night and God bless you!! I'll write to-morrow again sure.
>
>     Your always Geo.
>
>     Reguard to every body and mother.

January 26, 1918, was Dunk's thirtieth birthday. He started his letter to Eileen with a bit of humor by saying, "I hardly thot my birth day would ever be spent like this but some how thing have changed since, the Kaisers cow began to eat the shamrocks in Irland." (referring to Germany's Kaiser Wilhelm II). He then goes on to explain how Dad and Dunk's Wagon Company #3 is attached to the second battalion, which seems to be the next in line to be sent over to France, as the first battalion has already been sent "over there." He notes that the men have daily practice shooting on the rifle range. He also mentions that former President Teddy Roosevelt is scheduled to come to Camp Glen Burnie to give a speech.

Dunk, the boy from Western Montana, continued his letter by complaining about how he gets "tired of listening to Easterners talk 'jiberage'!" Finally, he sang the praises of Wagon Company #3:

> Believe me Wagon Co 3 is some Co. We have the best street in camp conseeded by every body, and objected to by several of the other Capt.s because they have'nt gotten they'er camps fixed up as good. How ever its' all on the outside and does'nt add any to our comforts

> only to the looks of the street. We have 20 tents, and a bungalow front fixed on each one of them so the front looks something like this [Drawing of a fancy tent with posts, ropes, stove pipe, portal front, door.]

From the end of January until February 12th Dad and Dunk continued their spartan existence at Camp Glen Burnie amid the heavy snow (often two feet of it). Dunk complained to Eileen of how hard it was to drill in these conditions. The cold continues so that he "can't think well" and it is so bitter that you "don't take clothes off in bed" with only three thin blankets. The knitted wool helmet, socks and wristlets that Eileen knitted for Dunk, however, keep him warm on the firing range and on guard duty and he is very appreciative. He ends one of his letters from this period with "I must quite or freeze."

Dad and Dunk continue to be in quarantine for mumps. Dunk explains to Eileen how during the final quarantine process they can't even write letters, so that she shouldn't worry if she doesn't hear from him for a while. She shouldn't worry about him either now or when he ships over, as he'll come back—"I've got to come back because of you." He also bemoans the fact that he didn't have enough schooling (just some high school/technical training) to become an officer, even though he has plenty of technical experience, but that doesn't seem to count for anything.

On February 12, 1918 Dad and Dunk left Camp Glen Burnie for Camp Laurel, also in Maryland, and one of the main camps for soldiers in the engineering regiments being sent to France. It was also a hastily-constructed camp by the U.S. Army Corps of Engineers for the overflow from Camp Meade and they had to walk from one camp to the other. As Dunk wrote in his letter that night to Eileen, "Well today we walked a thousand miles or more through the mud … but it's pretty warm so that helps a lot."

Soon Dunk cheered up because on February 20th he was made a corporal. He wrote to Eileen that he hopes "to go to training school to later become a sergeant." He also mentions that he is planning to take some French classes, and a week later even starts one of his letters to her with "Ma chere, Je t'aime." And then to assure Eileen he is going to be safe, he humorously writes, "And besides this wagon Co is so safe I'm almost ashamed to be attached to it."

Things continue to become easier for Dad and Dunk as February turns into March and the weather improves considerably. Dunk even tells Eileen that he is starting to enjoy the army life, as he has now has an office job which keeps him busy from 8:00 a.m. to almost 10:00 p.m. most nights and sometimes even to 1:00 or 2:00 a.m. He is working as a bookkeeper for the supply sergeant and they are in the process of outfitting all of the men at camp, so it keeps him very busy. Even better, he and the supply sergeant have a "nice big tent all to ourselves." And he has received his first pay check—all of $25.85 for two months (and enlisting) in the army—"That's the smallest Govt. money I ever got." He is proud of the job he is doing and hopes he can hold on to it so, "I'll be worth something in a mental way when I get back. This is great training, get me."

He finally received a letter from his father, too, and it cheered him up to know that his dad cared enough to write him. He continues to thank Eileen for all the woolen clothes she and her mother and sister have knitted for him and all the cakes they have sent him. He jokingly says, "I'm getting so indebted to you I'll have to get the Kaiser my self or I never will feel like I've did my part."

Dad and Dunk, as we know, enlisted in the Army and in an informative paragraph in one of his letters to Eileen, Dunk compares the conditions of the drafted men with the enlisted men:

> I expect the drafted men are sending all sorts of stuff home, but they have a chance, because they are in a regular city with all sorts of conveniences while we live in a camp that sprung up in a day, we have no picture shows here or elaborate Y.M.C.A.s but I hope when this thing is over it will be made up to the enlisted men for the hard ships he has to put up with while the drafted fellows are living at ease, (that is comparative). There

> is one place we'll have it on them how ever and that is we'll get to go over, while I doubt if the fellows in this second draft will get the chance.

He also notes in his March 5th letter to Eileen that the 23rd (Engineer Regiment) "seems to be different from all other organizations, every other Regiment has plenty of passes but we never have had them so you just save that bank roll Mother gave you and meet me in N.Y. when I come back."

Dunk and Eileen wish they could meet, but Dunk is never sure if he would get a pass to take a leave for a few days off, plus it seemed that the 23rd Engineers was scheduled for imminent departure to France. These lines from Dunk seem to substantiate the fact that American engineers were desperately needed in France to work on projects of all kinds ranging from building railroad lines and port facilities to constructing hospitals and army barracks to prepare for American troops. General Pershing was adamant in insuring that when the Americans reached France they would have the facilities and support they needed to successfully fight the enemy. And it was the American engineering regiments, including the 23rd Engineers, who would make that happen.

While Dad was in daily training at the camps and practicing military formations, Dunk continued to work fourteen to eighteen hour days as the assistant to the supply sergeant. He enjoyed this work and commented, "I'm still mighty busy and am forgetting every thing military I ever did know and I hope I never will have to remember any of it. This squads east and squads west don't appeal to me a little bit. I have'nt got a gun yet, but I issued my self a bayonet to-night I don't know what I'll do with it but they came in so I thot I might as well have one." But, like most others, Dunk, too, is eager to get out of the camp and go where he can do something patriotic. He'd like to be driving in the car with Eileen, but notes, "…when I pick up the Sunday paper and look at the headlines I'm glad I'm here doing all they will let me instead of burning gas over those good roads …"

Dad and Dunk are both hard working men, but Dunk, who is eight years older than Dad, has seen a bit more of life and has probably lived a bit more on the wild side. He lets Eileen know how the army is starting to reform him,

> Yes, I'm sure its' at least six years since we used to fight over poker games, and can you believe it I've not played two games since I joined the army. Shows what invirement does me an inveterate poker player converted from my evil habits of civil life by joining the army. I've not gone out with a girl or broaken any speed limits either. This army is sure some gay little reformer.

At Camp Laurel both Dad and Dunk felt the pace of military life heightening as March 1918 came to a close. For Dad there was even more military drilling and increased target practice. Perhaps he was able to arrange a two-day pass to visit his family in nearby New Jersey. For Dunk there continue to be long, long hours in the supply tent dispensing and recording equipment in preparation for the journey to "over there." Both men realize that their days on the home soil are numbered.

Sure enough, Dunk's next letter to Eileen written "In the shadow of the Statue of Liberty" on March 29, 1918, starts with "We're off …"

Dad's diary states:

**Left Hoboken 8:15PM 3/30/18.**

Dad and Dunk were finally on their way to war.

*USS George Washington* in Brest (CdI)

# Chapter 3: On the High Seas and through the Danger Zone

What was the two-week voyage across the Atlantic like for Dad and Dunk? How had they been prepared for it in their training camps in Maryland? They must have known that they would be passing through a very dangerous area—the eastern Atlantic off the coast of France—where the German U-boats patrolled looking for Allied merchant or army transport ships to torpedo.

Dad's diary simply states:

> **Left Laurel on Mar. 28 and arrived Jersey City 2AM March 29. Loaded baggage on barges and transferred it to transport (George Washington) at Hoboken. Embarked on transport 5PM 3/29/18.**
>
> **Left Hoboken 8:15PM 3/30/18.**

After months of basic training—for Dad four months spent at Ft. Slocum, New York and in a series of camps in Maryland: Camp Meade, Camp Glen Burnie, and Camp Laurel, Maryland; and for Dunk three months spent also in Camp Meade, Camp Glen Burnie, and Camp Laurel—they were finally on the transport ship that took them from Hoboken, New Jersey to Brest, France. The ocean crossing took two weeks.

Dunk's last letter to Eileen before his departure, written as he is about to board the transport ship, talks of a plan they'd apparently had to try to get married before Dunk left for France. Due to the uncertainty of the date of Dunk's departure, the plan never came to fruition. He assures her that he is in good company and has fine relations with his superiors. He also references the scene at the docks in Hoboken—the numerous trains and thousands upon thousands of soldiers that arrived in Hoboken to take the transport ships to Europe. It must have been quite a sight. This was the first international war that the U.S. had been involved in on such a major scale. American entry into World War I was to become a defining factor in the United States' rise to becoming a world power.

It is interesting to note that most of Dunk's letters are two pages written on YMCA "With the Colors" lined paper (U.S. flag on top left, YMCA in blue in red triangle on top right) which says at the bottom of the page, "Help your Country by Saving. Write on BOTH Sides of this Paper."

And so Dunk wrote to the girl he left behind, as he took his last look at the U.S. Note that this is the last uncensored letter that Dunk sent to Eileen during his army service. Once they were aboard ship and during their time in France, all soldiers' letters were censored, as can be seen by the censor's notation at end of each letter.

> In the shadow of the Statue of Liberty
> Mar. 29, 1918

Eileen Dearest:-

We're off, the Lieut. Just came in to our car and told Broten and I to take our last look at the old sand because, we were going right on board. We had expected to stay here for at least ten days before we went over but I guess we're needed now. I was going to write you a good long letter to post at the dock as this is our last chance to write when they wont be censored.

Honey I'm sorry I didn't have a chance to write you as I wish to, as it is we're pulling out now for the boat and in a little while we'll be on board. I can't write here every body is so excited, and we've been up all night in fact I've been up now for several nights almost all night but I guess I'm to excited to feel it when I get on that boat I'm going to sleep for a week. Even at that I feel fine. Dearest now the whole thing is over I know what we could have did, but when we left Glen Burnie we were due to leave in five days, then they raised it to ten days and from then on we've been ready to leave on 2 hr. notice. I've thot of this though every day since I came to Laural and I've wanted you here if we had just known you could have been in Laural and if you'd have consented we might have been married to. But what the use of talking about that now. I only want you to know I love you every bit in the world, and am mad to see you again Darling Girl. My letters have been bum I know but I could'nt write what

I wanted to when the Lieute was censoring them and when I know him as well as I do.

Not that I'm ashamed of my love for you, but I did'nt want it dragged through a lot of officers jokes. You understand don't you darling.

Dear you aught to see the trains here and the soldier thousands and thousands of them from every place all with packs and equipment. I've got no gun my self yet. They say they are going to make me a Sgt. When I get across and I'll get a pistol. This job of mine has been mighty heavy but its' payed I'm in strong with the "Top" and the Lieut. And Broten will do any thing for me he can. I'm his assistance, so we have things mighty nice along side of the rest of 'em for one thing I'm not a line soldier, and I only do about what my own judgment is. Must say Good-by Darling Girl I love you. Yours

George

Reguard and best wishes to every body and especialy Mother.

U.S. transport ships carrying troops to France were escorted across the Atlantic by cruisers, destroyers and torpedo boats equipped with hydrophones and depth charges, offering protection against the constant threat of German U-boats which tried to blow up both military and commercial ships. Throughout World War I the German and Austro-Hungarian U-boats sank or damaged thousands of Allied and neutral ships—both passenger and merchant ships carrying goods and war supplies. The most famous of these was the British liner *Lusitania* in May 1915, carrying both British and American passengers, but also almost 200 tons of ammunition bound for the Allies on the Western Front. Records indicate, however, that only two American troop transport ships, the *U.S.S. President Lincoln* and the *U.S.S. Covington*, were sunk and one, the *U.S.S. Mt. Vernon*, damaged. All of these incidents occurred off the coast of Brest, France, truly known as the "danger zone."

Dad had sailed across the Atlantic twice before—once as a boy of six and later as a boy of ten—both times with his mother who was returning to Scotland to visit her relatives. He had experienced the long voyage, far from any land, in a raging sea, and so knew what to expect. Dunk, on the other hand—a Montana boy—had never set foot in a boat, much less spent any time near the ocean, and his letter below gives us a good idea of how he, and probably hundreds of thousands of other young American doughboys (as American WWI soldiers were known), felt as they left their homeland for parts unknown.

On the High Seas. Some place in the danger zone

[no date, but probably the end of first or beginning of second week in April 1918]

Dear Eileen.

I'm having a nice time (?) have I been sick well I'd say so no more extended sea voiges for me. I just want to make one more trip on the briney deep and then I'm coming back to "Gods country", and where the real people live.

But when alls said and done this is'nt so bad after all. The sea has been fine nearly all the way over, and we have some real talent on board. Up to to-day I've not had any duties so I've had lots of time to think about you and all that you mean. I sure wish I was back wheeling the car over those good roads, and taking you out shooting squireals like we did last spring instead of going hunting Germans.

Well the censor is more strict than ever here so I can't say much. Only I'm well and eating every thing in sight. I wrote you a letter a few days ago but I'm afraid it wont go through. Inclosed you will find a ships paper, which will tell you all about it, if it gets by the censor.

I'd like to write you a hundred pages but you know I can't so I'm sure you wont blame me for not.

We expect to land in a couple of days more, you can guess how glad we will be to see land.

Our letters will be a long way apart from now on so keep up your heart "Little Girl" and remember every thing is all right any way

Address Me Wagon #3, 23rd Eng     As Ever

    A.E.F. Via N.Y.                                  G.W.D.

On the other side of the letter is "Censored by Lt. E.S. Overstreet, Wagon Co. 3, - 23rd Engrs, N:A."

The leaders of the American Expeditionary Forces (AEF) had spent months planning how to best organize the arrival of soldiers and supplies in France. They expected to send over two million men, so five or six thousand men were expected to arrive daily in French ports in May 1918 along with 10,000 tons daily of supplies. This was to be upped to six to eight thousand men a day and 20,000 tons of supplies by September 1918. But when the German offensives in early 1918 took place, the projections changed to five million men to come over with ten to twelve thousand per day and 75,000 tons daily of supplies. This was the target to be reached by July 1919. There were ten designated ports in France where the Americans were to disembark, the most important of these being Brest (where 791,000 disembarked), St. Nazaire (198,000), Bordeaux (50,000) and Le Havre (13,000). Americans also arrived in England—the most important port being Liverpool where 844,000 disembarked.

Dad and Dunk's voyage on a transport from Hoboken, New Jersey to Brest, France was by far the most common route to France for soldiers in the American Expeditionary Forces —almost 800,000 (43% of total AEF) arriving in Brest in 1917-18 and more than one million returning from Brest to the U.S. in 1918-19 after the Armistice. Brest had been chosen in early November 1917 as the best French port due to its extensive and well-protected outer harbor as well as an even more protected inner harbor—in addition to the fact that it had adequate port facilities and rail connections. The "rade," as the Brest port area was known, was like a large open lake area protected by points of land with only a narrow opening in the outer harbor, and by east, south and west jetties in the inner harbor, which gave it a major advantage over other French ports. It made the port large and secure. Even the biggest troop ships could anchor in the outer harbor and send troops in to port by tender, safe from German submarines.

To receive the American Expeditionary Forces (AEF) the port was upgraded and enlarged. The use of Brest by the Americans made it a world-class port. AEF engineers constructed more jetties (the total length of berths in all French ports built by Americans or acquired from the French in WWI in France was over seven miles), warehouses, restaurants, railroad lines, tent cities, prefab buildings, theaters, dorms, hospitals and prisons in the port area and adjoining parts of the city. From the beginning of the war to the Armistice Brest received 105 troop transport ships plus the hundreds of cargo ships that supplied the troops and brought war materiel. Even though there were German subs lurking around routes that led to Brest, only three transport ships were sunk or damaged and only sixty-eight lives lost.

Transport ships were painted in "dazzle" camouflage to cross the Atlantic so as to confuse German U-boats. This "dazzle" design combined with the color of the sea and sky and the up and down movement of the ships made it more difficult for German periscopes to accurately target the ships.

Two weeks on a ship, and for the majority of the men for the first time, must have seemed like an eternity. For the most part they could relax, but seasickness was a common malady for many. To keep the men occupied somewhat, most ships had a newspaper produced by those on board. Dunk references the paper in his letter to Eileen and, in fact, the newspaper he sent her did get through. *The Hatchet* of April 9, 1918 ("published on the High Seas") contained a British press assessment of the week's battles along the Western Front, concluding that the enemy had made successful gains along the entire front. It also contained some humorous poems by Missourians about their impressions of the sea, as well as comments on President Wilson's Anniversary War Speech (war having been declared by the U.S. on April 7, 1917) noting that "the only argument Germans will understand is the argument of force." The two-page paper ends with bits of humor:

> "Jack, what would you do if a torpedo bumped into us?"

*you might find good to read, Skip, this across the street. She has one too. Thanks.*

# THE HATCHET
Published On The High Seas

Vol. 2.　　　　　　　　April 9, 1918.　　　　　　　　Number 9.

## BRITISH PRESS COMMENTS ON WEEK'S WORK

ISLAND OF MALTA, April 9—The latest expected general attack has not yet arrived, it is believed, owing to delay of the Germans in bringing up heavy guns where needed. They will probably rely mainly on these when next attack is undertaken. London Times correspondent says prospect that enemy can create diversions somewhere in France continues to recede. Germans have hands full in new big salient. They are now in a less favorable position than they were a week ago.

Enemy infantry division made a number of attempts to advance along a front of nearly 30 miles. Fighting along course was heavy and enemy showed a great determination from early morning until late nightfall, infantry trying to get through our bombardments and machine-gun fire, but were severely repulsed.

Morning Post Correspondent says repeated attacks along practically our entire front yielded enemy such successful gains that his position in North Aise has been improved since last Friday.

## MISSOURI SHOWS US

We've heard from 'em—those Westerners who are willing we should print their Impressions of the Sea. The first to register is a Missourian. He bursts into verse, as follows:

### Byron Up-to-Date

Roll on thou dark and deep blue ocean!
But recently I took the notion
That since you've taken to your breast
These submarines, I'll take my rest
Calm and serene among the hills,
Besides, I'm rather tired of thrills.
In earlier days, ere I grew the wiser,
And you beamed kindly on the Kaiser,
I loved you well, but understand
That now I'm partial to the land
A pond, though small compared to thee
Is now quite wet enough for me
Henceforth, if I should feel I can't
Keep quiet and Museing start to rant—
I'll sing of ponds and creeks and such
That yet ain't hampered by the Dutch

### Moral

There's nothing in going to sea
That appeals to a person like me,
Deep sea navigation
Evokes the elation
A cow might enjoy in a tree.

The Editors regret that anything has slipped into print that was not original or proper credit given otherwise. The Slacker, in Monday's issue seemed almost too good to be true. We regret its space under the conditions.

Lost a bunch of keys port side. Return to Sgt. Room 145.

## THE PRESIDENT'S ANNIVERSARY SPEECH

NORDDEICH, GERMANY, April 9—(Trans Ocean Press.) Commenting on President Wilson's Anniversary War Speech, the following is published by the New York Tribune—"It has taken us a year to reach what the President in his anniversary speech at Baltimore defines as the moment of utter disillusionment. In that moment we perceive clearly for the first time the truth that the only argument Germans will understand is the argument of force. That the only thing they will respect is power that can crush them. A lengthy editorial concludes 'her designs of conquest and domination as we have said have been apparent from beginning of the war but to remove all doubt, even from honest minds in Germany itself, it was necessary that events should furnish concrete illustration of Germany's intentions and propositions."

Comment of the New York Sun. If in craven or traitor minds here or abroad, there has been a belief that the United States might compromise with infractions or strike a perfidious bargain with the betrayers of humanity, it can endure it no longer. The President has been patient with German statesmanship. Where his impatience has been misinterpreted, the misinterpretation has now been extinguished and the unalterable decision of the United States to win victory has been made so clear that not even Germany can misunderstand us. The President's speech is admirable in tone and is broad and big in its attitude. It is strong, convincing, inspiriting for our own people, for our Allies and for our enemy.

## SUNDAY'S SERVICES WERE POPULAR

Religious activities must be numbered among the most popular attractions aboard. On Sunday, the total attendance at services amounted to a full two-thirds of the entire ship's company. No little part of the credit for this is due the popular and energetic Ship's Chaplain, who has successfully coordinated the efforts of other welfare workers and thrown into the scale the full weight of his own forceful and winning personality.

## L'ENVOI

Just as the sun bowled into the western horizon yesterday our constant sister of port lowered her colors, and the other ships doing likewise. Then while we watched, she loosed from her rugged hip a white something draped with Old Glory. It plunged into the sea. Across the sun-shot waters came the faint notes of Taps. The ships sailed on. And that was all, save for the mystery lingering in our minds, and the sun melting into the sea's red glare like Egypt's pearls dissolved in holy wine.

"Full many a gem of purest ray serene
The dark, unfathomed caves of ocean bear"

The ship's newspaper (DY)

"Well, I'd try to see that everybody didn't faint so there would be somebody to carry me into a life-boat."

"Pack inspection! Alright, let 'er go. This once they ain't going to put us through a ten mile hike out in the country."

"Because we live below the water guess the cook thinks we can catch a fish. If our education was a little better we would try and join the engineers and get a square meal."

From this entry, it seems that the engineers were at the top of the heap and enjoyed the best conditions aboard.

The AEF also had army bands, and very likely there were daily band concerts aboard ship to keep the men entertained. Dad and Dunk probably joined in as some of the old favorites were played— "Over There," "Keep the Home Fires Burning," "Pack up Your Troubles," and "Tipperary." Religious services aboard ship were another popular draw, with *The Hatchet* concluding that at least two-thirds of those on board attended the Sunday service, with much credit given to the "popular and energetic Ship's Chaplain."

As Dad and Dunk approached the French coast on the U.S.S. George Washington they would have been in the most dangerous part of their voyage across the Atlantic. This is where the German U-boats lurked trying to prey on American transports and supply ships. With French assistance, the Americans sent out sea planes and dirigibles from Brest to look out for U-boats and to guide the transport convoys into port. The sight of these overhead meant that the coast was near and that soon, probably within a day, the men would set foot on land. One can only imagine how happy Dad and Dunk were to glimpse these welcoming aircraft.

French airship patrols for German U-boats and escorts U.S. transports into Brest. (ABMC)

Dad and Dunk would have been out on deck, along with the thousands of other soldiers, as the *U.S.S. George Washington* approached the "rade." What a welcome sight to know that they had made it across the Atlantic safely. After passing through the narrow channel between the two points of land, they were in the outer harbor. As the *George Washington* was the second largest transport used by the AEF, it would have moored in the outer harbor. Then, smaller boats or "tenders" would have come out to the ship to take the men, several hundred at a time, through the inner harbor to the docks.

In middle of April 1918, when Dad and Dunk arrived in Brest (a day before Captain Harry Truman, future U.S. President), General Pershing had ordered an increase in the number of men and supplies to be sent to the Front. For this reason the transport ships were in a huge hurry to return to the U.S. for more men and war materiel. By July 1918 an American soldier debarked at Brest every eight seconds and some days as many as 20,000 soldiers would arrive in transports. The tenders worked twenty-four hours a day to enable as many men as possible to disembark as quickly as possible so that the ships could return within a day or two, after being resupplied, to the U.S. As soon as the men disembarked on the piers in Brest, they marched off to Camp Pontanezen, a couple of miles north of the city.

This camp was really just a short way-station on Dad and Dunk's journey to the Front. Like many of their compatriots, they were to stay there only nine days.

AEF soldiers debarking at Brest. (ABMC)

Entrance to Camp Pontenezen, Brest, France, 1918. (CdI)

# Chapter 4: The Path to Pontanezen

For April 13, 1918, Dad's diary entry states simply:

> Arrived at Brest France April 13, disembarked and marched to Pontanezen Bks. Left there for duty at sorting yards April 16.

So Dad and Dunk were now *over there* in France. They were not yet in a war zone or near the dangers of the Front. As Dunk commented in his letters to Eileen they were in this "seemingly quiet peaceable land."

"Bridge of an ass"—that's the English translation, from the Breton language, of "Pontanezen"—the name of the huge American "rest camp" just two miles north of Brest, France where American Expeditionary Force (AEF) soldiers spent up to two weeks on route to the Front in northeastern France. Dad and Dunk, along with hundreds of thousands of others, would have marched up from the port, through Brest, and then about two miles north to this camp situated on an open windy plain and easily accessible to the fog and rain that came off the Atlantic Ocean.

The Pontanezen Barracks or "Camp Pontanezen" came to be the largest American camp in France in WWI. American and French officials had agreed in December 1917 on this site to be used as a temporary rest camp for AEF soldiers. The initial site was only a few acres in size and was the location of six Napoleonic-era stone barracks.

In the first few months of its use, conditions at the camp were not good. Barracks of corrugated metal, wood, and canvas were being built to house the expected 4,500 soldiers to arrive there, but the buildings were not sufficient and so tents were quickly put up to house the ever-increasing number of new arrivals. Often the tents had no floors so that men had to sleep on the muddy, cold ground. The camp at this time was poorly equipped, poorly run and had poor sanitary conditions.

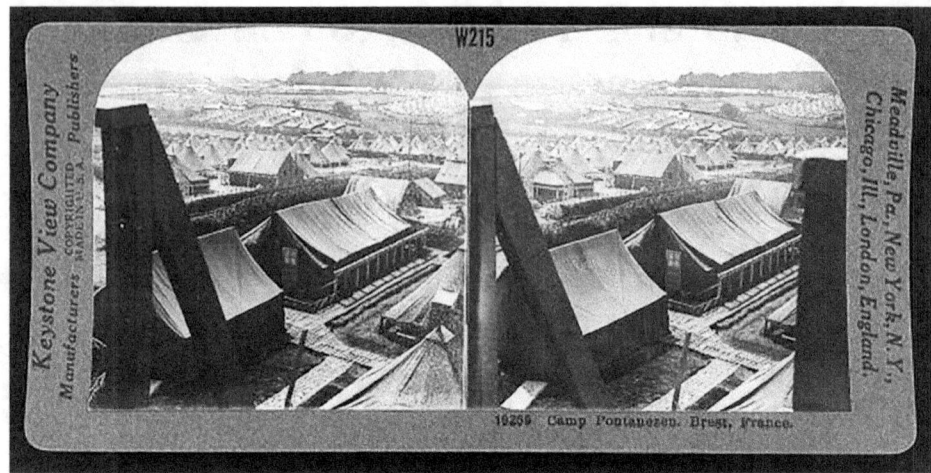

Camp Pontanezen, Brest, France, 1918 (LOC)

The number of soldiers arriving at Brest kept increasing and by the early spring of 1918, when Dad and Dunk arrived, the camp could take 15,000 soldiers. However, already by the end of May there were 42,000 there. At end of June 1918 more land around Camp Pontanezen was requisitioned, and work to increase its size began in August.

American engineers had the reputation of working well and quickly compared to the French. They made water tanks and reservoirs, dams, pumping systems, military camp barracks, fuel tanks, and renovated or built ports, warehouses, roads, bridges, railroads, and hospitals. By early September 1918 the new camp, now almost a square mile in area (600 acres), was opened to house 55,000 men, but it often had more. When finished it had 440 barracks for soldiers, 56 barracks and 56 dining rooms for officers, 18 kitchens and 18 dining rooms for troops, 179 latrines, 59 bathrooms, a huge supply depot, three stables, four auditoriums, one theater, ten officers clubs, a laundry , a delousing facility, a prisoner of war building, plus 4000 tents. According to camp accounts, the laundry employed 282 men in four teams and washed more than one million articles in June 1919 when soldiers returning to the U.S. passed through the camp. It was a city in itself.

There were rail lines inside the camp to transport supplies, three miles of paved roads and fifty-six miles of wooden sidewalks, called "duckboards." Water was obtained from a very deep well and from pumps in the nearby Penfeld and Izella rivers. And the camp used 450 horses that ate 5000 pounds of hay and another 5000 pounds of oats daily.

By the spring of 1919 each returning soldier had a bed with a mattress and could ask for as many blankets as he wanted. Showers could take 2,500 men per hour. The camp was totally electrified and had infirmaries and dental buildings. There was a sewer system and two fire stations, a YMCA auditorium which could hold 3000 men, and a woodworking/sawing factory at the camp to make beds, bureaus, benches, tables, toilets, tent platforms, ladders, turntables for trains, and boards for the sidewalks.

To keep the soldiers entertained there were baseball teams (inter-camp league played on Sunday afternoons) and boxing matches, an orchestra (also appreciated by French civilians), and YMCA huts for social and spiritual needs. In fact there were sixteen YMCA huts at the camp, one for each of the sixteen divisions of the camp. The YMCA huts mainly served food, but also lent books and magazines to the soldiers.

It was truly an amazing American village. After the Armistice and through the spring of 1919 with American soldiers returning home, engineers were sometimes building as many as twenty-six barracks a day so as to house the upwards of 82,000 men. Over 1,500 Brest civilians worked at the camp in transport, in the kitchens and at the laundry. In fact the American population at the camp was greater than that of Brest (67,000) at this time. There was even a train service from Pontanezen to Brest organized by the Americans.

So how would Dad and Dunk have experienced life in Brest during the third week of April 1918? They would have been very glad to set foot on solid ground, I imagine, after two weeks at sea. They probably enjoyed the march up to the Pontanezen Barracks, as they went through the city of Brest. Everything was new and different to these two young soldiers as they experienced their first few hours in France. They would have seen the huge port area with its multiple piers and large number

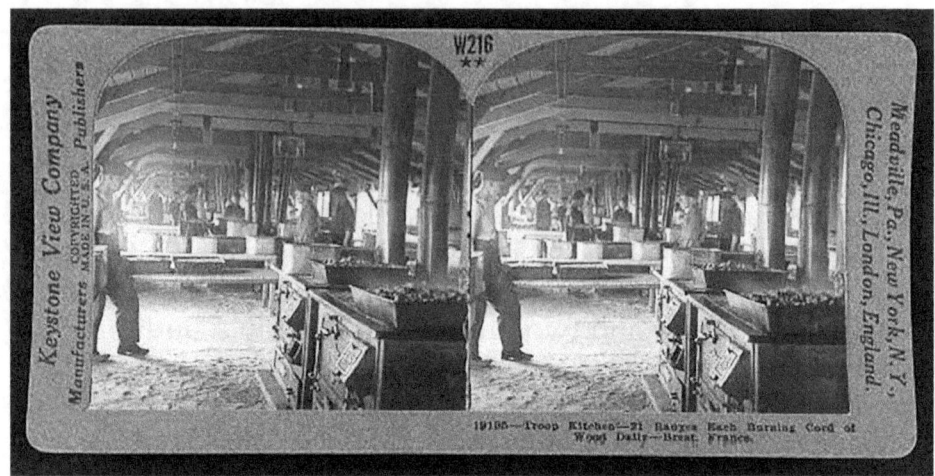

Camp Pontanezen troop kitchens with twenty-one ranges each. (LOC)

of warehouses, where enormous containers with food supplies, fuel, and war materiel were stored as they came off the ships prior to being sent to the Front by train. Many of the permanent dockworkers were from Black American regiments, but there were also crews of Chinese and Annamite (from French colonies in Southeast Asia) stevedores. Men worked around the clock unloading and reloading supplies so that the ships could return as soon as possible to the U.S. in order to transport more soldiers and supplies to France. Thus, it was vitally important that goods were sorted quickly and efficiently for forwarding onto the Front.

As Dad and Dunk went up the hill from the port they would have passed the ramparts of the city and the ancient chateau, dating from a third century Roman fortification, later updated in the seventeenth century by the famous French military architect Vauban. During WWI the YMCA had a huge welcome hut, the "Flag Hut," in the square in front of the chateau, which was a popular gathering place for American soldiers. It had the first self-service restaurant in Brest (with fresh eggs, unlike the army fare at Camp Pontanezen), a café, gym, showers, a barber, souvenir shop, 3000-seat auditorium, and a bureau to change money. The YMCA also showed films (estimated for 35,000 men per night in all of France), had dances and education courses, and offered free trips to parts of Brittany.

Typical films might have included *Freckles* (by Hollywood producer Jesse Lasky, starring Mary Pickford's brother Jack), *Cleopatra*, or more propaganda-oriented films such as *Heroic France, To Hell with the Kaiser, The Kaiser: the Beast of Berlin, Over the Top, The Unbeliever,* and *Johanna Enlists*. There were over thirty sports sites in Brest used by the AEF, so Dad and Dunk could have enjoyed tennis, basketball, baseball, biking, and boxing in their free time.

The view over the huge, protected port of Brest, known as the "rade," would have been seen to the west as Dad and Dunk marched toward the center of town. All along the route to camp Breton women would have been offering to sell them fresh strawberries, dried figs and other fruits, nuts, and handiwork. Little boys would have been running alongside the marching soldiers and asking for cigarettes, something to eat, 'bonbons' (candy), or maybe even a few "sous" (cents). Apparently the boys wanted to obtain cigarettes to send to their fathers in the French army, as French soldiers were poorly paid and did not have money to buy them. Children along the route would also occasionally break into song along with the marchers, very quickly learning "Hail, Hail the Gang's All Here."

After an hour or two Dad and Dunk would have arrived at Camp Pontanezen and have registered to enter. They would have been assigned a section of the camp and a barracks or tent. They would have learned the rules of the camp—when and where to eat meals; where to take a shower, use the toilet; how to take advantage of the leisure facilities, including the YMCA hut, which lent books and magazines and provided social activities including movies and religious services. They might have decided to join an intramural baseball team during the week they spent at camp.

Also, Dad and Dunk were both part of Wagon Company #3 (23rd Engineers Regiment) and so would have been assigned a work duty. Both Dad, in his diary, and Dunk in his letter to Eileen, mention that they had "sorting duty." This took place in the sorting yards at the port where many soldiers were tasked with dealing with all of the supplies piled up at the docks and in the warehouses there. They were given orders to separate certain kinds of freight (dry goods, refrigerated goods, war materiel, etc.) and place them in specific areas or vehicles which would take them to the railroad siding at the southeast end of the port. A special railroad yard with multiple tracks had been built by the AEF to facilitate movement of both supplies and troops away from Brest to the "intermediate zone" of central France, where the Service of Supplies (SOS) was located or to the Front in northeastern France.

Life in Brest beat to an American rhythm in 1917-19. It wasn't just the introduction of American jazz, ragtime, and the fox trot by the famous Black bandleader, James Reese Europe of the New York Army National Guard, but that new musical genre certainly did take the French by storm.

American soldiers were called "doughboys" (from the shape of the infantrymen's buttons which looked like flour dumplings or "doughboys," or because of their appearance after walking through dusty terrain which made them look as if they were covered in flour or dough), or "sammies" (after "Uncle Sam"). Their presence, in the hundreds of thousands, brought their lifestyle and customs to this previously rather provincial French town. They brought basketball, which continued to be played long after the Americans left, but they also brought a huge increase in automobile traffic to the narrow streets there. In addition to the doughboys' huge consumption of coffee and cigarettes, they brought American chewing gum to Brest. However, Dad wasn't partial to any of these items and Dunk only went for the cigarettes.

In the port area, aside from Bretons and Americans, there were Chinese and French Indochinese dockers and railroad workers. Some 16,000 German prisoners were housed in the Brest region; they helped with unloading supplies as well as working on farms to take the place of Frenchmen who were at the Front. Portuguese and Russians also passed through the city. The Russians had joined the war on the side of the Allies in 1914, but Portugal had remained officially neutral until conflicts between Portuguese and Germans over colonies in Africa brought Portugal into the war, also on the side of the Allies, in 1916. With all of these different nationalities passing through, Brest was a very cosmopolitan place in 1917-19.

The Americans certainly gave a huge boost to the local economy and, in most ways, this was a positive influence for the French. The AEF was very concerned with the morals of the soldiers and tried to inculcate white middle class U.S. values in the troops. This was done through training and then offering healthy choices at the YMCA and Red Cross facilities (no alcohol being served). But of course, drinking and getting drunk and causing trouble did occur, as did prostitution in some of the small villages near Camp Pontanezen.

How did Dad and Dunk react to what they saw in Brest? Dad wrote letters to his father in New Jersey and to some of his lady friends from his college days in Boston in which he described what he was seeing in France and how much of it seemed old fashioned. Dunk's letters to Eileen mention some of the new, strange sights and customs that they, as well as many other Americans, noted during their first few days in this new "old" country. Below, in his first letter to Eileen since arriving in France, Dunk assures her that he is safe and then goes on to mention some of the differences between French and American women, as well as the need to speak French in order to interact with the locals. Note the "Some Where In France" location—soldiers were not allowed to reveal their exact position—and Dunk's vague comments about his work duty; letters were not allowed to reveal details. At the very end of the letter you can see the name and approval by R S Morgan, apparently the censor for the 23rd Engineers at this time.

> "Some Where In France"
> Apr. 26, 1918
> 
> My Dear Girl:-
> 
> Some how time just get a way so fast you can't keep track of it, it seem like it was just yesterday that we landed in this seemingly quiet peaceable land for as far as we've seen so far it is just a big garden, and might just as well

be N.Y. State as France. So you see you must'nt worry about us, when you don't hear because its' just because, we're busy and most of the time we're busy in a way that its' impossible for us to write, such as being on the move or on some special detail work.

I spent a good long time on one of these details at the port where we landed with an other fellow, and if you had seen us you would have known why we had no time to write. Yes it was work but every thing was new and we enjoyed the whole stay. We meet a lot or rather saw a lot of French people. You can't meet people here unless you can "parliz-vous" or how ever you spell it. I have trouble enough spelling English let alone French, but you're a lucky girl you did'nt teach me any of your French or I'm sure I'd never gotten back.

The fellow who can talk French is right in it here.

Well to make it short, every thing is going fine. I just feel great we're sleeping out in tents, in a nice green field, how ever it's not very warm, the climate is inclined to be a little damp even at times, but its' not hurting us any.

I expect you can amagin all sorts of wild things now you know we're over safe, but you must'nt. The only diffrences is we spend more time thinking and talking about the folks back home and the good times we've had in the good old U.S.A. and telling each other how much nicer the girls are at home than they are here.

The other day I saw a Red Cross nurse and say she was homely as a hedge fence but those American clothes and American shoes sure did look good after looking at these funny dresses the French ware and their wooden shoes.

Well I guess I'd better quite this is getting long. I'll try to write oftener from now on, but I can't promise for sure.

Give my best reguard to Mother and the family and drop the word over to C.W.C.'s. Just call Dad up to and tell him I'm all right to won't you.

Well Dear this is a bum letter but its' about all I dare to write and theres such fuss around here I can't write or think. Every time I get a good thot some one comes in here and asks the millionth question and I forget what I had to say. So I'll just say good-night, and let it go at that.

>                               As Ever
>                            Geo. W. Duncan
>                            Wgn. 3. 23rd Engrs
>                       American Ex. Forces, France

> Ok
> RS Morgan
> 2 Lt Eben   name
> 23 Engr

Some days later, in his second letter to Eileen from France, Dunk complained about how his letters can only be "health reports" or talk about the scenery, due to censorship. He comments on the old French buildings and about his first time attending a Catholic mass and having to kiss the priest's ring. Dad and Dunk were both of Scottish Protestant heritage; they had never experienced such things. Dunk ends his letter with a yearning to be back home taking a spin in the car with Eileen. "Broten" and "Kelly" were both officers to whom Dad and Dunk reported. At this time both Dad and Dunk were corporals. They both became sergeants during the summer of 1918 while in Nevers.

>                        "Some Where In France"
>                                 Apr. 30, 1918
>
> Dear Girl:-
>
> It seems I'm very much in debt, I've got about four letters here to answer to you, but what the duce can I tell you. I don't want to make any more health reports as Broten calles 'em. But that and the scenery is about all there is. Except I went to church with the "Top" Sun. and after that we looked the town over, some towns these old places, if they were in the States they'd fall down and kill some one.
>
> Your surprised to know I went to church, well so am I, but Kelly was pioleting the party and steered in, it was a catholitic church built in the eleventh century and som, much a-granda. But the steam heat had been neglected since about the twelfth century so we pretty nere froze. It was a huge mass performance and the music was fine, also the priests had a very good argument with each

other, that I did'nt get the drift of very good. Then to make a very fitting finish on things Kelly lined up in a bad position and we had to kiss the priests or pontiffs or some highnessesses ring. Well theres strang things happen in this eastern land, but thats the strangest one on me yet.

Well quite a pleasant surprise just broak on us, all un benoence to me the regimental band just got into camp and struck up, "I'm in Love with a Beautiful Nurse." That's like a lot of other song stuff and poetry, there is'nt any such thing, that's why they write about 'em. Either that or then all the pretty ones are up at the front, its' a sinch they are'nt around here, you see I've had my weather eye out.

Well when I got here, the rush started and thus ended my attempt at writing for one night, this is no place to write letters to say the least so if I don't write very often please don't blame me to much. We're crowded here worse than we were before, and thats saying some. The supply tent and orderly is under one cover now, so your always trying to think three ways at once and you know I always have a hard time thinking one.

I must close this for now and get busy again. This is a beautiful day, I wish you were here with the car. I can think of nothing that would be more pleasant just now.

      As Ever

        Wgn. 3, 23 Engr.

        Am. Ex. Forces"

          France.

Row upon row of barracks at Camp Pontanezen, 1919. (CdI)

U.S. train engine type "Consolidation," one of 1,539 used in France, 1917-19. They were sixty-six feet long and weighed seventy-five tons. (PAN)

# Chapter 5: La ligne américaine — the Nevers Cut-Off

Dad and Dunk found themselves in a boxcar bound for central France after only nine days in cool, windy Brest. These railway boxcars, on which was written "40 hommes, 8 chevaux," were jokingly known as "40 men, 8 horses" and although they were a practical means of transporting as many men as quickly as possible, they were not the most comfortable form of transportation for American soldiers.

Dad's diary for April 20, 1918 reads,

> **Left Brest Apr 20 in a boxcar arrived at Nevers April 22 passing thru Le Mans and Tours. Marched to Sermoise Bks Apr 22.**

Nevers, a provincial capital in central France about 150 miles south of Paris, was in the "intermediate zone" and for the American Expeditionary Forces was a center for supplies and services needed to support the war effort. It was located in a safe area about equidistant from the Atlantic ports and from the Front. The ten major services that were organized from Nevers included the quartermaster, the medical-surgical, engineering, ordnance, the signal corps, the air service, purchasing, gas service, transportation, and the military police. The Nevers region would become known as the area where two of the largest American hospitals in France were being built—one at Mesves, just north of Nevers, and the other at Mars-sur-Allier about ten miles south of Nevers—each with 20,000 beds. Additionally, one of the biggest railroad engine repair shops in France was located in a suburb on the north side of town.

Speaking of supplies, engineering supplies for AEF operations in WWI totaled 3,000,000 tons and were valued at $450,000,000, which would be equivalent to some $9 billion today. These included both goods shipped from the U.S. and goods purchased in Europe from the French, British, Swiss and Spanish.

In terms of transporting men and war materiel to the Front, the rail line which passed through Nevers was a key element. Although General Pershing had requested that certain French railroad lines be dedicated to solely AEF traffic in order to facilitate the transport of AEF soldiers and supplies, this was not possible in Nevers. Nevers had only a couple of tracks and one railroad line entering town from the southwest (from the Atlantic ports) and a line leaving town to the southeast (eventually going towards the Front). These lines were used by both French civilian and military trains, so they could not be dedicated to the AEF. And because Nevers was on the most direct line from the ports to the Front, it was urgent that the Americans figure out a way to get around the bottleneck it presented.

And so the crucial "Nevers Cut-Off" or, as the French called it, "La ligne américaine" project was born. Dad and Dunk and the 23rd Engineers were to be one of five engineer regiments that worked on the Cut-Off — the most important railroad construction project in France done by the Americans during World War I.

This gargantuan project was in a planning and design phase from October 1917 to late spring 1918. A team of eight American engineers specialized in building railroads came in November 1917 to examine the landscape south of Nevers. They looked at the properties of the terrain and also took soundings in the Loire River to measure its depth in different locations. But it wasn't until April that preliminary work on the roadbed started and it wasn't until June 20, 1918 that the full-scale effort on the Cut-Off began. Then, miraculously, in only four short months of backbreaking labor, this rail project was completed. After October 20, 1918, AEF trains could bypass the bottleneck and delays in Nevers.

Most of the 240,000 engineers who served in France during the war had no prior experience in the military. After the U.S. entered the war in April 1917 the British and French asked the U.S. to give top priority to sending American engineers to France. And, indeed, American engineers headed up the

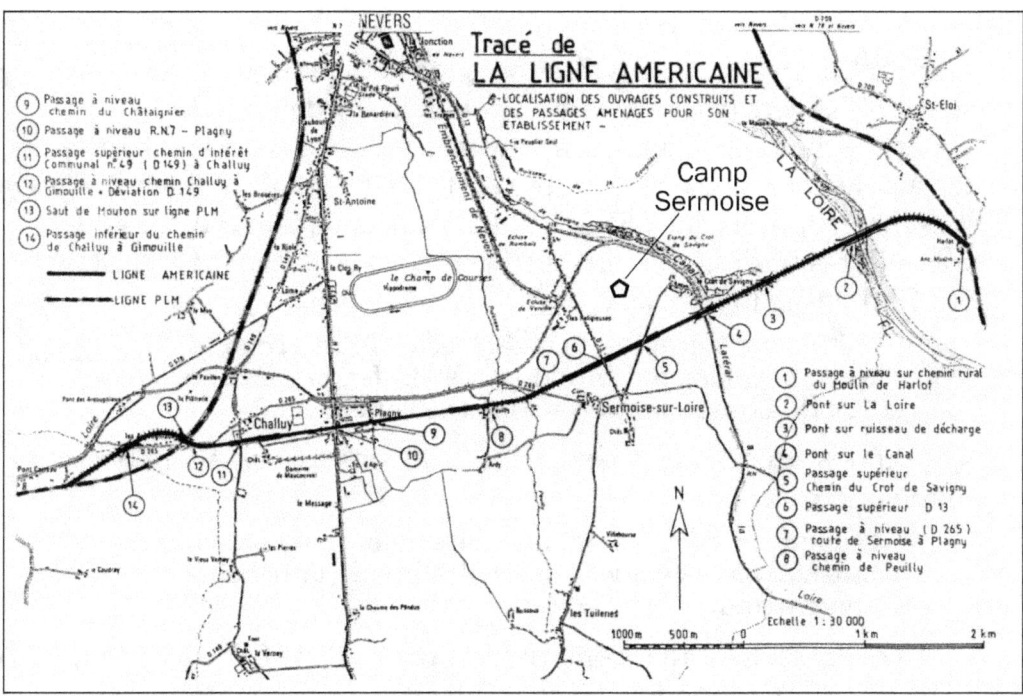

Map of 'La ligne américaine'/the Cut-Off showing railroad lines going to and from Nevers at top. (PAN)

construction projects in France that were essential for moving men and war supplies to the Front for the AEF.

Colonel Harry Burgess, commander of the 16th Engineers, was the man in charge of the complete Nevers Cut-Off project. The 23rd Engineers were under the leadership of Commander Fowler and were responsible for building the rail line on the eastern side—east of the village of Sermoise and toward the Loire River opposite the village of Harlot. The Cut-Off was an amazing project and was completed in record time. It was 5.5 miles long and connected the rail line coming into Nevers from Tours in the west to the line leaving from Nevers toward Dijon in the east. It shortened the route to the Front by over eight and a half miles—miles of congested rail traffic through the center of Nevers. Thus, the AEF saved many hours and days of precious time in transporting men and war materiel from the Atlantic ports of Brest, St. Nazaire, La Rochelle, and Bordeaux to where the war was being fought by the AEF in northeastern France.

As Dad's diary entry above states, after arriving in Nevers on April 22nd, he "marched to Sermoise Bks." The barracks were in Camp Sermoise, which was located about two miles south of Nevers in a very large open field bordered by the waters of the Loire Canal to the north and northwest and by the farm at le Crot de Savigny to the east. To the south of the camp was the proposed line of the Cut-Off. It seems that the project was still being discussed in April and early May, so that on May 5th Dad wrote in his diary:

> **Left Camp Sermoise, Sun. AM 5/5/18. Marched to Nevers. Quartered in old porcelain factory on the Rue de Gonzague overlooking the Loire River.**

But less than three weeks later, Dad was moved again back to the big project:

> **Moved on May 24 to new site near railroad on outskirt of Nevers where new railroad yd. is being constructed.**

Now it seemed that construction for the Cut-Off was about to begin. Preparation for the construction of this mammoth project took many weeks. Aside from the five AEF engineer regiments involved, which included almost 3,000 men, there were companies of Indochinese workers (from French colonies in Asia), a battalion of Italians, and two companies of Black Americans.

What did Dad, Dunk and the others in the 23rd Engineers have to accomplish as part of the team working on the most important American railroad construction project in France? How did they manage to do what they needed quickly and efficiently with the tools at hand?

First, and most importantly, the terrain where the double rail tracks of the Cut-Off were to run was in a relatively flat, low area near the Loire River and the Loire Canal. For this reason it was vitally important to build up a high enough roadbed to make sure that any flooding would not affect the rail line. To this end, the roadbed was designed to be some 120 feet wide and about 40 feet high in some areas. This necessitated huge amounts of dirt and fill to be brought in to the Cut-Off area for much of the five miles of roadbed. U.S. Army Corps of

Decauville locomotive working on the Cut-Off. (PAN)

Engineers documents state that 190,000 cubic yards of cut were made and 414,000 cubic yards of fill were needed for the project.

Dad and Dunk and others on the project would have used steam shovels to excavate the cuts. Then other machines, including a narrow gauge railroad using a small Decauville locomotive and small open hopper cars, were used to carry the hundreds of thousands of cubic yards of fill needed for the roadbed. A high timber trestle was constructed from which these side-dump cars loaded by steam shovels discharged the fill to save time. These American-made dump cars were the first of their kind in France. Wheel scrapers were also used, as well as 400 horses and over 3000 men. These earth-moving machines are all listed in French accounts of the Cut-Off construction.

Then there was the question of bridges to be built. The most important and most challenging was the bridge across the Loire River, just east of the village of Sermoise and east of the Loire Canal, which was worked on by several engineer regiments. This bridge was a trestle bridge over 2,000 feet long. The bridge supports were each made up of forty pilings placed together. The pilings were tree trunks that were sunk about twenty-five feet into the river bed with another twenty feet or so above the river to support the metal spans. Machines used included steam hammers to pound the pilings into the river bottom and cranes to lift the metal plates and pilings into position. Later, cranes were also used to position the rail lines on top of the

Nevers Cut-Off bridge across the Loire River (PAN)

metal plates. In one section of the Loire bridge, metal girders were placed between the supports which were thirty-five to fifty feet apart. Other sections were made up of fourteen-foot timber spans.

Other less challenging bridges included the one over the Loire Canal of some 215 feet, and a bridge overpass for a French railroad of 122 feet. There were also several grade crossings where local roads needed to traverse the Cut-Off as well as minor road or brook crossings. These were worked on by several of the other engineering regiments involved in the Cut-Off. When the construction yards were finally established at the two ends of the Cut-Off, on the west near the town of Challuy and on the east on the right bank of the Loire River near the village of Harlot, there were some 3000 AEF men involved in the project.

The local French inhabitants of the area south of Nevers where the Cut-Off was being constructed were absolutely amazed at the American "know-how," modern techniques, dedication, and speed of work on this project. All of this was happening at a very low point for the French due to German advances over the past few years, and so the enthusiasm generated by this project gave a big boost to French morale. Locals were also surprised by the rapidity and organization of the AEF camps in the project area. As one young Frenchman from Sermoise remarked about the camp where Dad and Dunk lived, "The American soldiers established their camp between the Crot de Savigny and the town. Besides the barracks, there were ultra-modern kitchens, shelters for many horses and mules, a veterinary clinic, and lots of supplies." Another young Frenchman spoke of the other American camp on the western side of the Cut-Off, "In less than two days the camp was set up. Nothing was lacking, including camp showers and a diving board on the canal."

However, a project like the Nevers Cut-Off also created some nuisances for the locals. The excavating, the boring, the drilling, and the frequent blasting did cause some unpleasant episodes for the inhabitants near the project. They were often told not to leave their houses on certain days at certain times due to blasting and the danger of falling rocks. Some residents were fearful that this project would affect the water in their wells, and to some extent this was true. In 1919 a couple of local wells showed a diminished output, but on the other hand another large well showed an increased supply of water.

Journalists from the local newspaper described the huge project and painted a picture of the peaceful fields now being excavated and with lines of steam shovels and light rail lines running through them. Work on the bridge across the Loire River necessitated harvesting hundreds of trees to form the pilings for the trestles upon which the metal plates sat. There was the constant sound of powerful steam hammers knocking the pilings into the river bed. Journalists also commented on the high quality of the work being done by the Americans and how their structures were "absolutely secure." Locals continued to comment on the modernity of machines and equipment used: steam shovels, steam hammers, cranes, air compressors, various locomotives to pull the hoppers with fill, huge winches and centrifuge pumps. This equipment represented the height of progress to the French living in the area.

Dad and Dunk worked long hours on this project, and for Dad, it had a profound influence on his later career as an electrical engineer for American railroads. But all was not work: Dad and Dunk enjoyed their days off as we learn in diary entries and letters from their time in Nevers.

There was a large farm at the Crot de Savigny, near the American camp in Sermoise, built in the 15th century. One day Dad and Dunk slipped out of camp and went there. Dunk relates this to Eileen in his letter of May 4th, "We had a feed of scrambled eggs, and got some butter and milk. We took our own bread with us that we hooked from the cook house because they can't sell you bread here every body gets what they need but they can't sell any to the soldiers."

The farmhouse and kitchen made quite an impression on Dad and Dunk, and Dunk vividly described them to Eileen, "This place we went to was a great big stone house and the kitchen was big enough to put a bungalow in side of. There was a big fire place but they had a range to cook on in front of that and to one side of it was a charcoal stove. They use more charcoal here than wood. The thing though that took my eye most was the stone floor, and the copper and brass cooking untencils, all shined up till you could see your self in them and the wooden shoes all lined up in a row by the kitchen door." He goes on to say that this was a rather exceptional farm in that they had quite a number of German prisoners working on it and a lot of nice stock. He also mentions what a difficult time they had trying to make their hosts understand English, and bemoans the fact that he and Dad did not speak much French. Dad, being a science and engineering student at MIT, had studied German.

Dad and Dunk lived at the old porcelain factory in the center of Nevers for about three weeks in May and during this time took advantage of what the town had to offer. Nevers was a medieval city, still encircled with stone walls and containing many old stone buildings. For a boy brought up in the West, where the houses were all made of wood, this was a novel sight. Dunk commented in his May 10th letter about how everything

Farmhouse at Le Crot de Savigny, where Dad and Dunk had a meal, near the American Camp in Sermoise. (JBP)

was old, including the seats at the picture show that he and Dad ('Doug" in the letter) attended, and how things in France were fifty years behind those in the United States.

Dunk had now been away from Montana for six months and just yearned to return to the country and people he knew and loved. He wrote to Eileen:

>On Active Service with the American Expeditionary Force
>
>May 10, 1918
>
>Dear Girl:-
>
>Well things have quited down now, I guess every body has gone up town so I'll try to get a few lines writen to you. I got off this after noon at 3:00 and went up and had a grand bath in a tub some treat believe me, and then we walked around for a while and looked at the walls and the store windows. The store windows here are a joke any little store back home sports a better glass front than the best of 'em here.
>
>Well we finaly ended up by getting a big omelet, and a lot of French fryed spuds and some green peas all of which cost the three of us 22.00F francs or about $3.96 American collateral but then its cheap at half the price.

We enjoyed it very much.

Well, again, I'd give all Uncle Sam owes me and give up this job any time if I could be back going out this spring instead of H.A.C. not discouraged, no, not atall but there is better places than this in the world and the best place is out there in Western Mont.

Last night Doug. and I tried a picture show. We got the best seats in the house and they sure were'nt any thing to brag on. Don't think I'm partial its' not that atall its' just the country ther'er 50 years behind in every thing, believe me the Americans have the right idea when they build a thing it's not built so it wont come down, and whats more it comes down when it gets out of date here they build every thing of stone and it stays for a thousand years.

I've just been reading some of your letters over again I can't seem to make my self believe that at one time not so very long ago I was there with you missing breakfasts and staying up two thirds of the night and eating suppers at mid-night it does'nt seem possible that was me, that does every thing so agrivatingly prompt and to the letter now.

Of course we can go out nights here and stay as late as we want to just so we get in by 9:00 oclock and get to bed by ten.

The Kodak book has'nt reached me yet but it will come along some of these days Kelly got a box last night that was sent to him after we left Laural.

Don't you worry about this German drive or me getting into it. I'm beginning to think I'm not going to have a chance to get that helmet for you I heard a captain say to day he did'nt think we'd ever see the front, and all the French people here we talk to seem to be sure it will be over in three or four months. That aught to be encouragement enough for one time so I guess I'd better turn in Good night.

|  |  |
|---|---|
|  | Yours |
| Censored by | Cpl. G. W. Duncan |
| Lt. E.S. Overstreet | Wgn. Co. # 3. 23rd Engrs |
| Wagon Co #3, 23rd Engrs. | Amex Forces, France |

AMERICAN Y.M.C.A.

ON ACTIVE SERVICE WITH THE AMERICAN EXPEDITIONARY FORCE

May 10, 1918

Dear Girl:—

Well things have quited down now, I guess everybody has gone up town so I'll try to get a few lines written to you. I got off this afternoon at 3:00 and went up and had a grand bath in a tub some treat, believe me, and then we walked around for a while and looked at the walls and the store windows, the store windows here are a joke any little store back home sports a better glass front than the best of 'em here.

Well we finally ended up by getting a big omelet, and a lot of French fried spuds and some green peas all of which cost the three of us 22.⁵⁰ francs

> or about £3.96 American collateral but then it's cheap at half the price, we enjoyed it very much.
>
> Well, again, I'd give all Uncle Sam owes me and give up this job any time if I could be back going out this spring instead of H.A.C. not discouraged, no, not atall but there is better places than this in the world and the best place is out there in western Mont.
>
> Last night Doug. and I tryed a picture show, we got the best seats in the house and they sure weren't any thing to brag on. Don't think I'm partial it's not that atall it's just the country they're 50 years behind in every thing, believe me, the Americans have the right idea when they build a thing it's not built so it wont come down, and whats more it comes

First two pages of the original letter of May 10, 1918 from Dunk to Eileen. (DY)

Another day Dad (Doug) took it upon himself to write a letter to Eileen Wagner so that she would get mail. Dunk apparently didn't have enough time to write her for several days and Dad wanted to make sure that Eileen would keep getting letters.

In his next letter to Eileen, Dunk referred to Doug as "a loyal good kid." There was an eight year difference in their ages. At this time, Dunk was thirty and Dad was only twenty-two. As we know, Dad had lost his older (and only) brother when he was eleven years old, and perhaps Dunk fulfilled this role. And Dunk had no brothers, only two younger sisters who had been ostracized from the family for going off with the "wrong" men. So, he too, was perhaps glad of a younger brother figure in his life.

In Dunk's letter of May 26th he commented on the long hours they work. He could not describe their project (the Nevers Cut-Off), but he wrote, "This job we're on here they say is one of the most important jobs going on in France, in fact it's figured as next in importance to the front line."

> Some Where In France
>
> May 26, 1918
>
> My Dear Girl:-
>
> I've got two dandy good letters from you which I wanted to answer several days ago but I've been sure the busy "home" believe me.
>
> Your last letter was a wringer and it came just at the right time. No I was'nt blue not by a long shot, I was too busy to be blue and things were breaking to good for me. You remember I always got just about any thing I wanted in civil life, well its' the same way here. I'm on my old job again only on a much larger scale. I'm incloseing a picture of my nicest pet on this job you might show it to C.W.C. and H.A.C. and tell 'em I'm running a job now what am, I got a boost and I practically have two Cos. Under me here, also we've moved since I last wrote you to an other safe place, and just as nice and quiet as the last one. This job we're on here they say is one of the most important jobs going on in France, in fact it's figured as next in importance to the front line. "Nuf sed".

Dear I'm awful sorry about that good box being sent back believe me we needed it bad to, never the less I want to thank you ever and ever so much for all the money you spent and the trouble you went to to send it to us. I'm sorry to because I can't request it We can't ask for any thing now according to the latest dope. Its' sure too bad after all your hard work knitting to but you just save 'em till I get back I'll need socks then to I hope.

Poor Dear that uncensored letter was'nt half as much of a letter as I intended to make it had I known how soon we were going to sail.

Never the less you just must read between the lines in these and remember every one is written with just the same sperit as that one was, only more so. The more I see of people here the more loyal I become to the folks back home, and the more I care for you.

Doug has a letter here he wrote a few nights ago to you when I was to busy to write and he thot you should have a letter. He sure is a loyal good kid and tells me its' time I was writing to you about every other day wheather I've go the time or not. You may think I should or could burn a little midnight but they wont stand for that at 10:00 we must turn in and at 5:00 we must turn out and then we work 10 hrs. and believe me we work.

Well Good night Dear I must close and turn in.

Sgt.. G. W. Duncan
Wgn. Co. 3: 23rd Engrs
A.E.F. France

To describe the conditions under which letters from WWI France were mailed, I describe below the envelope in which many soldiers' letters were sent, including the May 26, 1918 letter above of Dunk, to which Dad (D.M. Burckett) must have also contributed. Soldiers were not allowed to say where they were in France, nor were they allowed to refer to any military matters, nor say exactly what they were doing. All letters were censored, in this case at the company rather than regimental level.

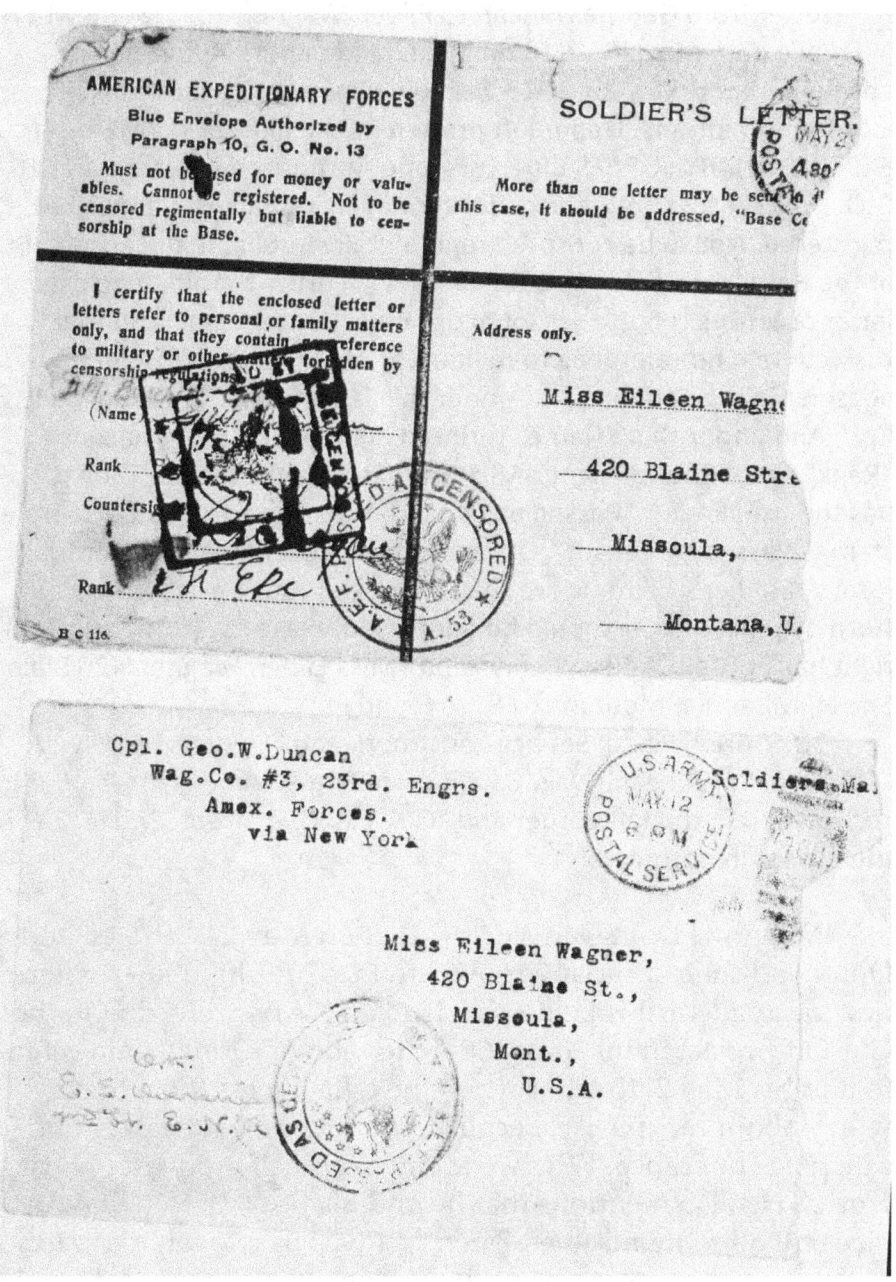

Example of censored mail in WWI. (DY)

Letter from George Duncan to Eileen Wagner from "Somewhere in France date May 26, 1918 on plain lined paper (2 pages) in envelope dated May 29, 1918 with blue lines on front dividing it into four quadrants. Upper left printed in blue ink says "AMERICAN EXPEDITIONARY FORCES Blue Envelope Authorized by Paragraph 10, G.O. No.13. Must not be used for money or valuables. Cannot be registered. Not to be censored regimentally but liable to censorship at the Base." Lower left in blue ink says "I certify that the enclosed letter or letters refer to personal or family matters only, and that they contain no reference to military or other matters forbidden by censorship regulations." Just under this is signature "D.M. Burckett, Cpl." And under that "Name" (printed in blue ink) G.W. Duncan, "Rank" Sgt., "Countersigned" R S Morgan, "Rank" Lt ERC. Then it has the usual A.E.F. "Passed as Censored" stamp and another purple stamp "Passed by Censor". On right top of envelope in blue print it says "Soldier's Letter More than one letter may be sent in th..... (torn off) this case, it should be addressed, 'Base C... (torn)". Bottom right has printed "Address only" and "Miss Eileen Wagner, 420 Blaine Street, Missoula, Montana, U.S." is typed in.

"U.S. Army Postal Service" postmark and "Soldiers Mail" with "Cpl. Geo. W. Duncan, Wag. Co. #3, 23rd Engrs., Amex Forces. Via New York" typed in top left corner and "O.K. E.S. Overstreet, 2nd Lt. E.N.A." the censor in bottom left.

We know, from Dad's diary, that on May 24, 1918 he and Dunk and their company moved to the Cut-Off area—"where new railroad yard is being constructed." After referring to the Cut-Off project in his May 26th letter above, Dunk again refers to it in his May 27th letter where he tells Eileen "Don't you worry about me, please, because I'm in the most healthy and safe place in France. Why we are'nt even using powder on the work." He also mentions that he and his boss, Broten, have a nice tent all to themselves. Then he gives us a lovely description of the French countryside in the spring—"... the other day when I was cutting across a field of some kind of French flowers. The fields here are sure beautiful in the spring, in fact its' a most beautiful old country... " But it also reminds him of home and how much he misses Montana and his times there with Eileen.

In Dunk's May 27th letter to Eileen he again talks of "an other big works" which would likely be one of the large American hospitals built just north and just south of Nevers. Again, due to censorship, soldiers were not allowed to mention where they were or to mention any place names in their letters—hence "somewhere in France" is often at the top of Dunk's letters. This is why the combination of Dad's diary entries, which although brief do mention place names and dates, with the more descriptive letters of Dunk, allow us to piece together the real story of where they were and what was happening.

Another "health report" is how Dunk starts his next letter to Eileen on June 2nd, but then he admits that there was some excitement in camp due to an "air-boat." That is what Dunk calls an airplane, as he explains the novelty of seeing this "air-boat" land in a nearby field, and then later in the day take off again. He reckons that after this war "air-o-planes will be as common as autos." He then again tells Eileen that he's not sure he'll ever see the Front as he's needed on the project (the Cut-Off) he's doing in the "SOS" (Services of Supply—as the Intermediate Zone around Nevers was known as). He mentions that there are 550 men on his part of the project and four times as many on the other side. These figures are consistent with what other sources state in terms of men working on the Cut-Off.

Dunk then waxed poetic about how he another soldier walked up a country road that evening and sat on a bank near some woods and listened to the birds – something he'd never done before. He comments that "We're as peacable as an egg omelet."

Some Where In France<br>June 2, 1918

Dear Girl:-

Well here goes for an other health report. Thats about all my bum letters amount to, but I guess thats better than nothing, is'nt it? We did have a little excitement though to-day when an air-boat came busing along and lit in a grain field near here. We see them every day but theyr just student plains, nothing war like about them at all. This one had two officers in it and they came over and asked directions to a place or too and then came back this evening and sailed away, just like we'd clime in to a jit and roll away. When this wars over air-o-planes will be as common as autos.

We get but very little news here from the front, but what we do is pretty good I think and most of the boys are betting on some dession by Sept. as for my self I doubt if I'll ever see the "Front" they need this work done back here in the S.O.S. and it look like we'll be the birds to do it.

I wish you could see this country now where we are its' out in the Proviences of course and every place you go is little farms and long low stone houses. They are cutting the hay now and theres flowers by the millions lots of Roses. It seems a shame for such a bunch of savages as us to come into a pretty country like this and wake it up, with our hundreds of moter trucks and and modern machinery, tairing through things.

On this job I'm on now there is no less than five hundred and fifty men. You can amagin whats happening, while just across the way a short distance is about 4 times that many.

To-night Kelly and I took a walk up a country road for a mile or so and sat on a bank near some woods and listened to the birds sing. Can you amagin me a warrier doing any thing as tame as that in such a war as this. I expect you would rather be expecting me to say I got drunk on carbolic acid, and tore down a stone wall, but nothing doing on the rough stuff. We're as peacable as an egg omelet.

Oh! by the way I had a peace of apple pie last night since I've gotten to be sort of first assistant to the "Top" I get in on "things", you know. Well the cook put one over and invited us down when we got through work about 11:00 o'clock and we sure enjoyed our selves. It was the first one of its' kind I've taisted in almost 6 months, can you believe it?

Well after telling you all this its' hardly nessary to say I'm feeling great, and the weather is the finest ever, just right. "Gee Whize"! I'm raving about this country am I not? Well you got to give the "Old boy his due" any way. At that I would'nt give a sixty foot lot on Blane St for the best farm they've got if I had to live on it.

I must turn in so I'll close hoping to hear from you very soon again.

Reguard to Mother, and the rest of the family, and to your self; well every thing.

As Ever Yours

> Sgt. GW Duncan
> Wgn Co 3, 23 Engrs.
> A.E.F. France

(O.K. C.M. Hurlburt, Lt. ERC)

Dad, Dunk and some of their company were living near the city of Nevers and so on Sundays they sometimes went into town for a meal at a local restaurant. French meal customs were somewhat different than American ones, and Dunk found some of it strange:

> Last night Kelly and I went down town and had supper, and believe me it was sure good. This is the way it went. A girl brings in a chunk of black looking bread and lays it on the table not on a plate. After we enjoyed looking at that for a while she brough in some fish which we enjoyed eating with our bread then she brings in some nice little peaces of roast beef, and some mashed potatoes, which we put away then came tea and I enjoyed it best. Can you amagin what a shape I'm getting in, the change in the army has made in me I mean. Then came a big bowl of lettuce we dipped into. I thought it was all for us and was begining to think I'd struck some thing to fill up on, when low and behold she comes and grabs it away, and hands it to an other table. "Can you beat it?" say Kelly. "I can't says I." and we sat back and waited a while and in came some nice cheese and nuts, and an other slice of bread a piece. And says Kelly, "They call this an American

> institution." And I agreed with him that they were all rong and we payed about .90 Amex. Coin a piece and walked, feeling pretty well satisfied at that.

Dad, meanwhile, was taking advantage of his days off in Nevers to go on long hikes with some of his buddies to see the countryside and to visit surrounding towns. Often they walked over thirty miles a day. Diary entries from May, June, and July 1918 describe these outings.

> **May 23, 1918: Hamer and I hiked to Pougues-les-Eaux a watering place for mineral baths. Here are the springs St. Leger and St. Leon. Some very beautiful places there. A fine view of the Loire can be obtained from the café at Belle-Vue. Distance hiked about 33 m.**
>
> **June 9, 1918: Hamer and I attend procession (Catholic) at Varennes at estate of Marquis Albert de Lenferna.**
>
> **June 16, 1918: Hamer and I hiked to Challuy about 14 mile hike.**

Challuy was the village at the western end of the Cut-Off where construction was just beginning to take place. As we know, the whole double track, five and a half mile project, including the major Loire River bridge as well as several smaller bridges, was completed in only about four months of construction. Prior to the actual construction, of course, there had been several months of planning. In Dunk's June 9th letter to Eileen, he mentions what a nice construction camp they have right next to a "big steamshovel cut." He seems to be very happy with his job, finally has some space of his own in his "office," and is well liked by all the others in the company. He goes on to comment about the popularity in France of American rag time music — a bit of Americana brought over to France in WWI. Dunk then notes how the Brits get their cigarettes carefully wrapped up and hidden in rolled up newspapers. It seems that cigarettes were some kind of contraband. Most Brits, however, still smoked pipes, as did other Europeans. Cigarettes, due to their size and ease of lighting compared to pipes, really came into their own during WWI. It was much easier and safer to smoke a cigarette at the Front in a trench, than to be constantly having to light up a pipe. After WWI even women started to smoke cigarettes. What a revolution.

> Some Where In the S.O.S. France
>
> June 9, 1918

Dearest Girl:-

Its Sunday morning and I've just finished reading over a bunch of your letters you've written me since I arrived over here they sure are good, sort of make Sunday seem more Holy as it were. Its' sure a good thing to find something to make it see more as it should, though I never was much on sunday at this time of the year. I'm afraid though you'll think this isn't a nice place from the sound of my beginning.

It is nice here it's the nices construction camp I ever was in. We have a nice little shack for an office right on the side of a big Steamshovel cut we are working in, and I have a table of my own in it, and believe me its' my table so every body steers clear of it, and don't fool with any thing around it. I think I must be getting to be a regular crank, and yet there is'nt a man in the CO. would'nt do any thing for me, I don't believe.

Of course we are'nt doing any fighting, but that's not our faults, and we wont get any crosses for bravery, but the other day our 1st Lt. called me up and told me I'd handled my end of this job so well he had desiced to take me with him on some other work. I guess its' a whale of a job and so much to do on it I don't know how I'll get along, but if it goes through I'm going to tackle it any way. I never was afraid of a hard job any way. I'll tell you more about it when I get there if I have a minute to my self.

The Lt. is away looking up the job now to see how many men we can use to start with, and when we can start. He thinks it will be about the middle of next week, and will last about three months so you won't have to worry about my well fair for at least three months more, and by the way the boys are hitting the line now it may be over by then _ _ _ _ _ _

Ma Chere;

Since I started this letter I've been down town with Kelly for dinner and supper and we took in the show besides. I didn't care so much for the show but the musice was great, you aught to hear these French people warm up to good old American rag time. They played three or four peaces and showed some Amex Light Artilary, on the march, and you aught to have heard them aplode it was great.

As for the dinners they don't amount to much except the price which was 5.00F each or about .90 cents U.S.A. and believe me that a lot of money when your only getting about eight dollars a month, but I'll get a little more next month. Those poor cigeretts they have hard luck don't they. You know once I had a fellow working for me from England and every week he used to get a couple of boxes cigeretts neatly rapped up in a weekly paper. They took the cigeretts out of the boxes you see and distributed them evenly over the paper and then rolled it up so it looked just like an ordinary harmless paper.

I received you last most welcome letter just thirty one days after it was written May 9th some long time between letters now is'nt it and when I get on this new job it well be longer still because I'll be away from the Co.

Kelly was asking after you when I got your letter and some way I happened to tell him you had a flunk on versification. He's quite a poet him self, you know and he said, "Well what the duce does a pretty girl want to write poetry for any way." I agree with him to.

Why Chere, (how my French I saw that in the picture show to-day) I can't request any thing any more they wont let us, so you'll just have to save all those nice things you've made for me till I get back or perhaps Christmas they may let us receive boxes and you can send 'em then, and many many thanks for all your kind thots and hard work on my behalf.

Some time ago you asked me what I did with my other watch I don't know if I told you or not but I have it yet, how ever as soon as I can arrange it I'm going to sent it to you.

Well regards and best wished to every body, and tell C.W.C. I hope he's better again. I'm mighty sorry to hear he's been sick.

This letter is'nt a bit good Honey but I've had to stop about ever other line to tend to something else. This office sure isn't any place to write letters.

Tell Mother she sure is all right. I agree with her every time.

As Ever Yours

> Sgt. G.W. Duncan
>
> Wgn Co 3, 23 Engrs.
>
> A.E.F. France

(O.K. C.M. Hurlburt, Lt. 23rd Engrs)

It is interesting to note that this June 9th 1918 letter was the last letter Dunk sent to Eileen until after the Armistice (November 11th), or at least the last letter that made it to her, some 5000 miles away. He did send Eileen a telegram on July 8th saying only "Safe, well." Most likely he was working in an area where there was no easy access to pen, paper or a way to mail letters. As he often commented, he was putting in very long hours and was often too exhausted at the end of the day to think about writing a letter. His telegram, probably costly to send, shows that he still cared deeply for Eileen and wanted to let her know that he was in good shape.

In July 1918 work on the Cut-Off was proceeding apace. But holidays were holidays. What does an American WWI soldier do to celebrate his national holiday in France? Dad's diary tells us:

> **On 7/4/18 went down to Nevers in AM. Hamer and I went to Y.M.C.A. and saw movies in P.M. Stayed to 11 P.M.**

Maybe because this was the Fourth of July holiday, the soldiers didn't have to be back in quarters until after the usual nine p.m. curfew.

The YMCA (Young Men's Christian Association) along with the Salvation Army, were two of the most important American organizations to provide social activities and a "home away from home" for the soldiers of the American Expeditionary Forces. The YMCA had been founded prior to the Civil War, and in that war it began offering services to support the morale and well-being of the soldiers. In WWI the services of the YMCA expanded substantially. There were morale/welfare/recreation (MWR) activities. There were rest and recreation (R&R) programs for battle-weary soldiers. There were also the YMCA canteens or "huts" and overseas exchanges during WWI where soldiers could buy or get coffee, candy, cigarettes and other American goods. And then there was entertainment—movies, dances, shows. The YMCA truly lived up to its reputation of being a "home away from home."

General John Pershing had asked the YMCA to take enormous responsibility for moral and welfare services. In addition to the MWR, R&R, and canteen services above, the YMCA provided troop education, as well as facilitating things like stationery for soldiers to write home on (seen on some of Dunk's letters to Eileen) and mail services. There were 26 R&R centers in France during WWI along with 4000 "huts" for recreation and religious services.

The YMCA served over 19 million soldiers of the Allied armies, including almost 5 million American soldiers and sailors both at home and overseas, in all regions of Europe as well as in Africa and Asia. Of the 26,000 paid YMCA staff, over 13,000 of them were sent to France. There were an additional 35,000 volunteers who saw to the spiritual and social needs of the 4.8 million American troops. After WWI there was an institutional shift of responsibility for the human services rendered by the YMCA; they were assumed for the most part by the military itself. Non-profit organizations, however, still fill in some of the existing gaps in military human service programs.

Dad's diary entry for July 9th simply states:

**Tues. 7/9/18 started in work as Co. Clerk.**

At this point Dad changed from being a "blue-collar" soldier to becoming a "white-collar" paper pusher. He was no longer mainly planning and building roads or railroads but rather keeping track of the company's supplies and where they came from and how much they came to and to where they were being sent. Dad was always very methodical and kept accurate records, and was well-educated, and so it is not surprising that he was chosen to be the company clerk for the 3rd Wagon Company of the 23rd Engineer Regiment. This job, apparently, still left him plenty of time to go hiking all over the countryside on the weekends on both day and overnight hikes. Dad uses the word "American" instead of the word "English," that we would use today, for the language they speak.

> **Sun. 7/14/18 Hamer and I walked 25 miles. Passed thru Guerigny and Urzy. Most of walk thru woods. Stopped at house of Frenchman who talked American well.**

> **Hamer and I started hike Sat. P.M. 7/20/18. We hiked 15 miles that night. Slept under hedge along road. Had no blankets or shelter. Up 4:30 A.M. hiked thru St. Jean aux Amognes, St. Benin D'Azy and Imphy and St. Eloi and Nevers. Total hiked 44 Mi. or 72 Km.**

Dad was very organized. Aside from writing in his diary, he wrote scores of letters during 1918. We know this from the pages at the back of his diary where he logged in all the letters he wrote as well as the ones he received. From late June through July 1918 he wrote fourteen letters and received fifteen; in August he wrote nine and received seven; in September (during the St. Mihiel and Meuse-Argonne Offensives) he was very busy at the Front and so only wrote two and received three. For October, November and December the figures were eight and twenty, seventeen and eight, and fourteen and twelve. The majority of his letters were to his father as well as to several of his lady friends from Somerville, New Jersey, where he grew up, and from the Boston area during his MIT years. He even wrote two to Dunk's girlfriend, Eileen, toward the end of 1918. Unfortunately, none of these letters survives.

On Dad's days off, either by foot or on bicycle, he managed to see both of the huge hospitals being constructed in the Nevers area, as he notes in his diary entries below. The hospitals were being built to each accommodate 20,000 sick and wounded. The trip to Mesves was made by bicycle with a buddy and on dirt roads, so forty-five miles made them quite tired.

> **July 26, 1918: "On Friday Hamer and I took a 45 mile bike trip out to Mesves in order to see some of the detached men about allotments. It was a great trip but we were pretty tired when we got home. We started at 1:30 PM were home by 9 P.M. Got wet on the way home. Helped guide a truck train thru town. On our trip we passed thru Pougues and La Charite. The later town was very interesting, there being the ruins of an old church. At Mesves there is under construction a large hospital.**

> **July 29, Monday Kelly left this P.M. for Eng. Officer School. Sorry to see him go as we had been together since Meade in P-106.**

Kelly had been a more senior soldier in Wagon Company #3 and often mentioned by Dad. As noted, they'd been together since their training at Camp Meade, Maryland in December 1917.

The Nevers region in central France, as previously mentioned, was the center of the American Army's SOS (Service of Supplies). It was here that huge enterprises were set up to support the AEF. This included providing for the troops for the duration of the war. Hence the reference in Dad's diary below of picking up six tons of flour in the village of Sancaize to take to a bakery in the village of Magny.

The other hospital in the region was about ten miles south of Nevers, at Mars-sur-Allier. Dad's visit to the wounded at that hospital was probably his first close encounter with the horrors of war. These were the lucky ones who had made it off the battlefield and, after several days on a train, to an American hospital in a safe zone. If they didn't die of their wounds and weren't cut down by the terrible influenza outbreak in 1918, they might make it home alive. It's hard to tell what kind of an impression the visit with these wounded American soldiers had on Dad. He was a man of few words, who did not show emotions easily, and certainly did not record feelings about his visit in the diary entry.

On his way back to Nevers he got a ride with a "Frenchy." Dad was brought up in a strict family where drinking was probably frowned upon, and even during my youth I never remember him drinking much at all, so having to "be cordial" and accept the "glass" from the Frenchy must have been a fairly new experience for him.

> **Sunday Aug. 4, 1918 Hamer and I started on hike. Met O'Rourke in truck and went to Saincaize to get 6 tons flour. Took flour to bakery in Magny and then went to Amer. Hosp. at Mar-sur-Allier. Looked place over and talked with wounded fr. Soissons – Chateau Thierry front. Fine location for hospital. Walked part way home and got ride with a Frenchy. We had to stop three times and get a glass. Hated to do it but one has to be cordial. Frenchy brought us right to camp in wagon.**

Now we return to the reason the 23rd Engineers were in Nevers—the construction of the Cut-Off. Dad and Dunk were, at this time, working on this project as company clerk and aide to the supply sergeant respectively, although it seems that

American Hospital in Mars-sur-Allier

occasionally both of them were seconded to others jobs. Work on the Cut-Off had started in June and was in full swing until the project was completed and trains began to run on it on October 20th.

The new rail line was used extensively during the last month of the war, often seeing up to ten supply trains and five troop trains a day. This would be approximately equivalent to 5,000 tons of materiel and 5,000 soldiers passing along the Cut-Off daily. It was used even more extensively after the Armistice to return troops to the Atlantic port cities for the voyage home. From November 11, 1918 to August 12, 1919 there was an average of three trains a day with returning American soldiers. Figures state that this included 735 trains, each transporting 1000 to 1,500 men back to the Atlantic ports for the voyage home.

The Nevers Cut-Off stopped functioning as a necessary rail line in late 1919. By 1921 the French government had passed a law requiring that war projects no longer needed be dismantled. And so, by 1925, "la ligne américaine" was dismantled and the rails sold. The bridge across the Loire River was taken down and the pilings were cut off at water level so as not to impede the river's flow. Boat traffic runs on the Loire Canal which runs roughly parallel to the river, so river pilings would not have interfered with commercial shipping.

Today, a hundred years later, what remains of the Nevers Cut-Off? The roadbed is still visible, rising above the flat riverine land, although of course mainly covered with grasses, bushes and some trees. The pilings are still visible at low water in the summer from the banks of the Loire below where the bridge crossed the river. The rails are gone, but at the farm at the Crot de Savigny by Dad and Dunk's former work camp in Sermoise, the current farmer's grandfather had been given a few bits of rail. These were recently gifted to a local historian who has had them made into a memorial to the Americans who built the Cut-Off. The memorial was inaugurated in November 2017 to commemorate the hundredth anniversary of the Americans coming to help the French in WWI.

The time spent in Nevers by Dad and Dunk was far from the Front. During these months, late April to late August in 1918, the majority of American soldiers had not yet entered the front lines. Yes, American soldiers had fought assisting the British (at Seicheprey on April 20, 1918) and reinforcing the French in the Marne area (with American offensives at Cantigny, Soissons, Château Thierry and Belleau Wood in May-June, 1918) and suffered terrible losses, but it was not until September 1918 that the Americans had their own command of a sector. The American First Army formally took charge of the attack on the St. Mihiel Salient southeast of Verdun on August 30. The battle that pushed the Germans out of the salient took place from September 12 to 16. After that General Pershing immediately marched the army back to Verdun to take part in the Meuse-Argonne Offensive (along with the French Fourth Army to the west). The Meuse-Argonne Offensive turned out to be the push that ended the war; it began on September 26 and continued until the Armistice on November 11, 1918.

Dad and Dunk were about to join these American First Army attacks.

Ruins in Verdun, 1918 (DMB)

# Chapter 6: Off to the Front in Verdun

Next stop the Western Front—Dad and Dunk were finally on their way to the front line. The train trip covered about 200 miles but took four days. How did they feel after the long months of training in the U.S. and then the almost five months of work on the Cut-Off in the safe "Service of Supply" zone in central France? Getting outfitted with a gun, a gas mask, and a helmet in the town of Is-sur-Tille certainly must have been a reality check—a sign that they would soon be in the war zone where their lives would be endangered. Were they anxious about what was to come, about the fact that they were going into the fray? Or were they excited that at last they were going to see some action? Neither Dad in his diary nor Dunk in any subsequent letters mentions any fear of what they were about to experience at the Front.

Dad's diary entries simply state:

> Left car facilities yd. Aug. 26, 18 and entrained for front at 6:30 P.M. Arrived Dijon A.M. 27 and Is-sur-Tille that afternoon. Outfited with gun, gas-mask and helmet here. Laid over 1 day and 2 nights here and left Is-sur-Tille A.M. 29 and went thru Chaumont and arrived St. Dizier about 5 P.M. Laid in St. Dizier till 9 P.M. and left for Rattentout.
>
> Arrived near Rattentout 7 A.M. Aug. 30.-18. Detrained at Ancemont 1 P.M. Went into Camp at Cinq Freres same afternoon. Camp is situated in a woods on a high hill between Ancemont and Senoncourt. A great many rats about billets.
>
> On Sept. 4 Sgt Woods and I walked over to Verdun and back. No people living there but soldiers. Most all of them live in underground tunnels. City pretty badly shot up. Walked over in 1 hr. 40 min.

It is interesting to note that they arrived at their camp at Ancemont, about five miles south of Verdun and seven miles northwest of Saint-Mihiel, on August 30th, the same day that the American First Army formally took charge of this sector of the fighting. The American push to retake the Saint-Mihiel Salient,

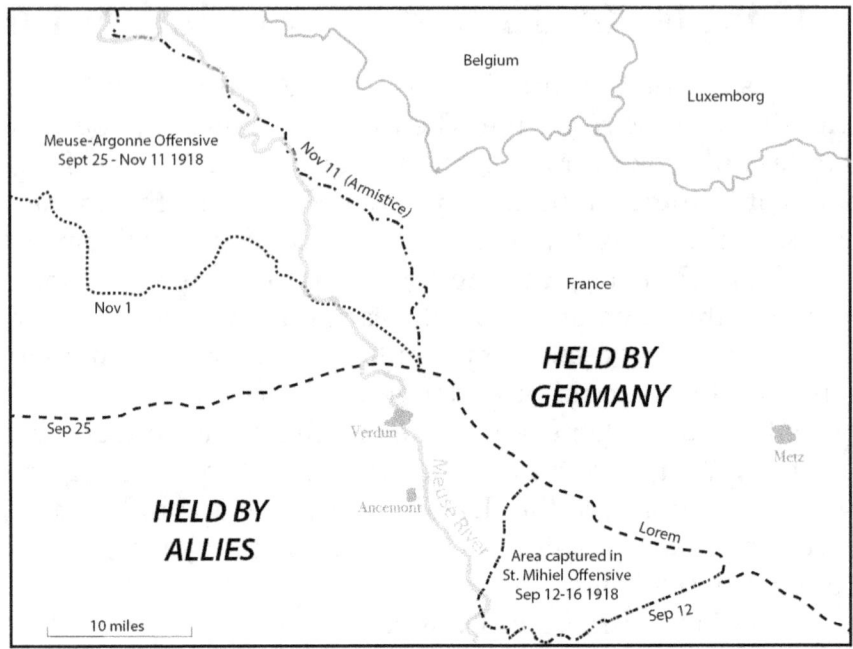

Greater Verdun area, northeastern France.

just to the southeast of their camp, would take place less than two weeks later, from September 12-16, and thus they were well positioned to take part in this first major American battle of the war.

    Conditions at Camp Cinq Frères ("Five Brothers") sounded pretty dismal. Many of these camps had been set up quickly without much thought as to sanitation or proper food storage. With lots of rats living around the camp there was always a chance for disease to spread. Conditions in Verdun proper, however, seemed equally bleak. The city had been almost totally destroyed by German shelling during the ten-month siege in 1916—the famous Battle of Verdun. Although the French had defended the city, it was at great cost. Because the war continued in 1917-18 with the Germans less than five miles away from Verdun on the heights to the east side of the Meuse River, positioned for continued shelling, there was no chance to repair the destruction. Civilians were gone. The soldiers, as Dad describes, were often living in underground tunnels

Water tower on top of Citadel, Verdun, destroyed by German bombing, 1918. (DMB)

or in the underground part of the Citadel—the huge, mainly underground, fortress that housed thousands of troops and included a hospital, a chapel, laundry facilities, kitchens and bakeries. It was like a self-sufficient underground city.

The Saint-Mihiel Salient was land held by the Germans that jutted out from their territory to the Meuse River at Saint-Mihiel, about twelve miles southeast of Verdun. The Saint-Mihiel Offensive, intended to reduce this salient, was the first independent American-commanded mission. General Pershing, commanding general of the AEF, now had an army of nearly half a million men. Pershing had persuaded France's Marshall Foch that the Americans should be given their own sector of the Western Front. And so, on September 12, 1918, the thrust to push the Germans out of the Saint-Mihiel Salient began, with sixteen U.S. divisions, some 400,000 plus troops, supported by French artillery and French tanks and a mixed force of Allied airplanes taking part. This operation, which totally surprised

23rd Engineers Regiment repair a road near Verdun, 1918. (ACE)

the Germans and cleared them out of the salient, lasted for only five days, including just thirty-six hours of intense fighting followed by clean-up operations which ended on September 16.

What would Dad and Dunk have been doing during this time period? They arrived at their Ancemont camp, within sight of Saint-Mihiel, less than two weeks before the offensive began. As the 23rd Engineers were a road engineering regiment, they were undoubtedly tasked with inspecting the state of the roads, noting where repairs needed to be made, and then completing the repair work. The 23rd consisted of four battalions of engineers with three companies each, ten truck companies of thirty-one trucks each, and five wagon companies consisting of sixty-one wagons each. Thus over 3000 men from the 23rd Engineers, along with engineers from other battalions would have been involved in this essential work.

Dad and Dunk were in Wagon Company #3. As road engineers they would then have been heavily involved in preparing and repairing the roads leading into the edges of the Saint-Mihiel salient to ready them for the upcoming AEF attack. Many of the roads had not been used by heavy vehicles since the Germans had taken over that area in 1914. Due to previous heavy shelling, however, as well as heavy rains, the roads were washed out and in terrible condition in many places. There was no time to order large shipments of fill to be brought to the Front, and so the 23rd Engineers had to use the rock from broken stone walls and destroyed houses to fill in

Soldiers carry logs to fill in holes in road, 1918.
(ACE)

the roads as they went. Much of this work was accomplished through manual labor using horses and wagons, but there were also large trucks and bulldozers to help in road reconstruction. Once the offensive started, Dad and Dunk and others in their company would have been right behind the front lines continuing to fix up the roads as the army marched forward.

As Dad states in his diary below, on the third day of the offensive he and some other sergeants went up to inspect some of the territory recently taken from the Germans, less than six miles from his camp. This was probably just after the thirty-six hours of most intensive fighting had ended. Again, the engineers were desperately needed to keep the roads in adequate condition for the tanks, heavy vehicles and supply wagons to move in both directions as the AEF chased the Germans back toward Germany.

> **September 14, 1918: Sgt. Broten and I and Sgt. Sutton went up to recently reconquered territory beyond Mouilly taken by Americans in drive started Sept 12, 1918. Went thru German trenches and dugouts.**

What must Dad and his buddies have thought as they went through some German positions? World War I, since the autumn of 1914, had basically turned into a trench war. There was little territorial gain for either side in four long years, despite huge losses of soldiers on both sides. Both armies had dug trenches and fought from them by occasionally "going over the top," a move usually preceded by a huge artillery barrage. So when Dad and his buddies inspected the recently-occupied German trenches, they must have seen what living conditions had been like for the German soldiers in the front lines. Because the Germans had a more complete light railroad system in the Verdun and Saint-Mihiel battlefields than did the French, the Germans were able to get supplies, such as cement and other building materials, to the Front more easily than the French. This enabled the Germans to build better, less destructible, more comfortable and safer trenches and dugouts than the French had. Dad and the other members of his company must have marveled at the quality of the Germans' battlefield living quarters. Amazingly, many of the German cement bunkers, blockhouses, trenches and gun supports are still in evidence to this day.

Immediately after the September 12-16 Saint-Mihiel Offensive was finished, the AEF First Army, as promised by General Pershing to Marshall Foch, returned north to Verdun (on the Meuse River on the southeast side of the Argonne Forest) to ready itself for the Meuse-Argonne Offensive, which was to be the decisive battle to end WWI. Pershing shifted his half-million men, including artillery and tanks, of the First Army by night. They had to move twenty to thirty miles over poorly constructed railroads and even worse roads. And this, too, is corroborated by Dad's diary entry for September 17th.

> **September 17, 1918: Tuesday, broke camp and left at 9 P.M. for parts unknown. Last night bombs dropped on both sides of us. Rode bicycle part way and hiked rest of way. Clouded up soon after we left. We passed near Luemmes and thru Rampont and Dombasle to wooded section No. East of Dombasle. It was raining quite some by the time we hit a place to camp about 4:30 A.M. As soon as daylight Connolly and I put up shelter half and slept till 1 P.M.**

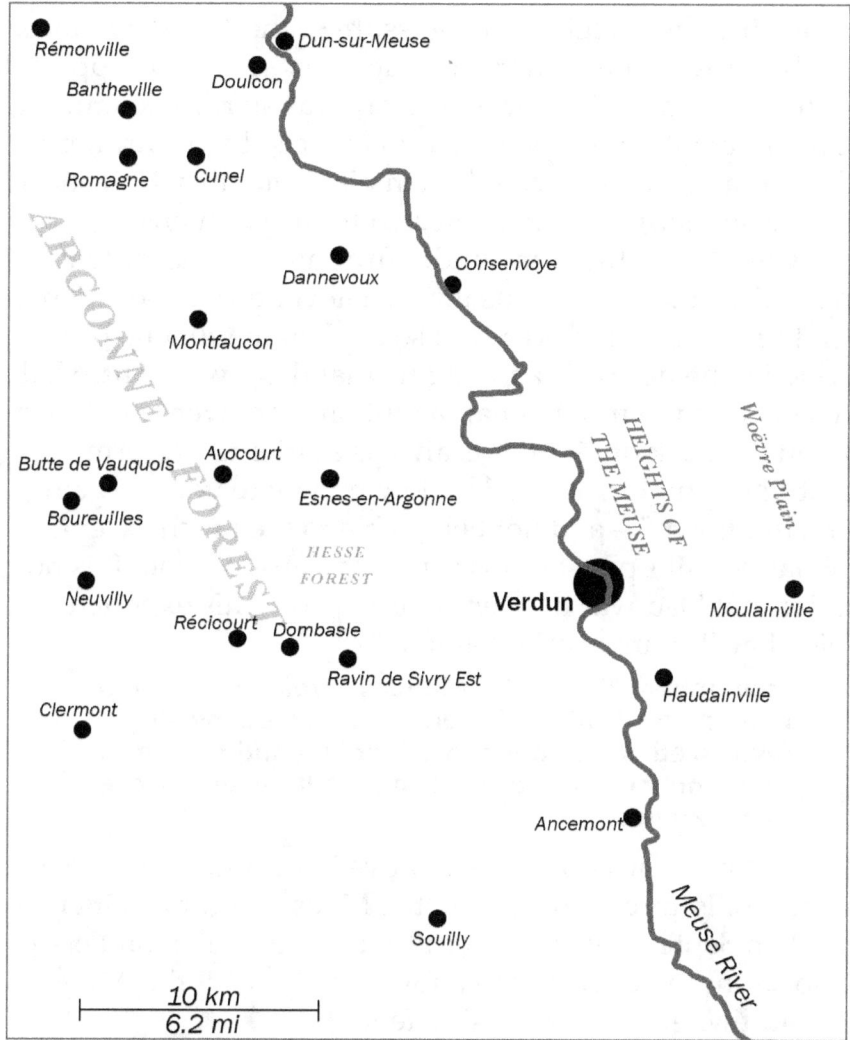

Map: Dad's diary mentions these locations in the Meuse-Argonne area of northeastern France.

**September 18, 1918: 1:30 (P.M.) broke bivouac and piloted wagon train to new camp southeast of Dombasle on main road. Just after we arrived Fritzie started dropping a few shells just over our heads. My 1st time under fire which hardly can be called a time. Name of Camp Ravin de Sirvy Est.**

So now Dad and his wagon company were less than five miles from the German lines. By this time, after retreating quickly from the Saint-Mihiel salient a few days earlier, the

German army was feeling the pressure of the Allied advance. Now that fresh American troops had been added to support the British and French, the German Army was starting to crumble. It still had plenty of firepower, as evidenced by the artillery shelling that Dad commented on in his September 17th and 18th diary entries above; 'Fritzie' referred to the Germans.

It was Dad's "first time under fire" and he was probably unnerved by it. It also seems that whatever orders he had been given to more forward were not so explicit in what he was expected to be doing. I can imagine that there was controlled chaos involved in moving half a million men twenty to thirty miles in the dark of night. It is always scarier to perform operations at night, not really knowing where you are going—"parts unknown"—and not being able to see much except for what was lit up by bombs exploding around you. It is no wonder that Dad was not very happy about this experience—"which hardly can be called a time."

> **September 23, 1918: Monday broke camp and moved to vicinity of Clermont. Moved by night. Bivouaced at Camp Prevost for night and moved to permanent camp in afternoon Tuesday in pine grove Camp Prevost.**

Dad's next move, recorded above in his diary, five days later and only three days before the Meuse-Argonne Offensive started on September 26th, was also by night. General Pershing did not want the Germans to know exactly what the AEF were doing and where they were situated.

> **September 26, 1918: Drive in Argonne started. Broke camp – moved up. Passed thru Neuvilly north of Clermont.**

Finally. The Meuse-Argonne Offensive, a combined American-French operation which was to end World War I, got underway at 5:25 a.m. on September 26, 1918. The road north from Clermont-en-Argonne to Varennes-en-Argonne, a distance of some ten miles, passed just west of the Butte de Vauquois. Dad mentions his camp north of Neuvilly, which would have been less than two miles from Vauquois, an important hill held by the Germans and eventually taken by the Allies with many casualties. His company was most likely working on this important road heading north, as it had been heavily shelled by the Germans in an attempt to stop the Allied advance. In fact, just north of Neuvilly at a village named Boureuilles, there was a huge bomb crater that had completely obliterated the road. Dad's company probably had been working to repair the road so that Allied troops could proceed further north during the offensive.

The next day, September 27th, however, Dad's most important news was not about the war, but rather about the fact that he has been promoted to sergeant. Indeed, he has been a sergeant for almost two months now, but the order appointing him took over a month to reach him in wartime France. Dunk had been promoted to sergeant in May in Nevers, three months earlier, so I imagine Dad was now eager to be entitled to the same number of stripes as Dunk wore on his uniform. Also, there was probably a small raise in pay. In any case, this note of personal interest took precedence over any war stories on the second day of the Meuse-Argonne Offensive.

> **September 27, 1918: Order received apt'd me as Sgt. (RSO#171 Aug. 22/18 to be effective fr. Aug. 1st 1918).**

Heavy fighting continued through the end of October in the Argonne Forest. The Allies had penetrated the first two German lines of defense, but the third and final line was not overrun until the end of October. The Germans were putting all the men they had against Pershing's attack there and so there were huge numbers of American casualties, but nothing compared to the slaughter of British and French troops earlier in the war. General Pershing, following President Woodrow Wilson's orders, had been very right to insist upon having the large majority of American troops fight together as a unit only under American generals. If this had not been the case, if they had been allowed to fight alongside French and British troops before the full AEF entry into the war, many more American troops would have died.

> **September 29, 1918: Broke camp north of Neuvilly this A.M. and moved back to Camp Ravin de Sirvy. Arrived their 1 P.M.**
>
> **Left camp to rejoin Company Oct 7. Jackson and I walked over most of France but finally located the bunch near Esnes on road to Avocourt.**

Since September 17th Dad had moved five times in less than two weeks. At times it seems as if he and just a few others from his company must have been sent to specific areas to accomplish specific tasks. The war was still raging not more than a few miles north of where they were camped. Perhaps the various wagon companies of the 23rd Engineers were spread out to different areas to continue the constantly-needed road repairs as the American First Army advanced. In any case, Dad and one of his buddies, Jackson, had been separated from Wagon Company #3, and as Dad notes, had a difficult time reuniting with the company. In WWI there were many anachronisms. Modern war technological advances such as tanks, airplanes and radios were just coming into use in WWI, but Dad and Dunk worked with horses and wagons—remnants of a previous era. So did Dad and his buddy Jackson have use of a radio or did they find their way back to their company by asking others on route? If the latter, then no wonder it took them quite some time to find their home company.

> **On Oct. 18 moved again from near Esnes to camp in Hesse Foret near Dombasle. Jackson and I have dugout attached to office. Good location only quite muddy. Have a horse of my own now and have to curry it every A.M. and have to feed it.**

Finally after a month of living like gypsies, Dad and some of his company moved to a more permanent camp at Verrières Farm in the Hesse Forest, part of the larger Argonne Forest, northwest of Verdun, between Dombasle and Esnes—about three miles from each of these villages. The Meuse-Argonne Offensive continued, but the fighting, still very heavy, was now much further north. It seems that Dad was now again performing his duties as company clerk.

Verrières Farm in the Argonne Forest (JBP)

There was a farm at this location, but the owners had long since fled due to the war. Dad's camp was in a protected wooded area just north of the farm, and the dugout, where they slept next to the attached office, was in an underground shelter made of corrugated metal with a wooden door and covered with earth and bushes. There were a couple of very basic bunk beds and a small wood stove for cooking. Having a horse of his own meant that Dad could more easily get around the forest on trails and on the very muddy dirt roads.

By the end of October, after five weeks of desperate fighting, the AEF and French had pushed the Germans out of the Argonne and substantially north of Verdun along the Meuse River. In the first eleven days of November the American and French forces raced north chasing the Germans out of the Meuse Valley. The Germans knew that the end was near and by now they were basically in retreat.

The 23rd Engineers were among those regiments assigned to the Chief Engineer of the First Army of the AEF during the

Meuse-Argonne Offensive. During the last days of October and in early November there were twelve engineer battalions, consisting of over 16,000 men, involved in roadwork in the Meuse-Argonne area and in building temporary roads in the former "no man's land" in the AEF First Army area. The 23rd Engineers had almost 3000 men involved—more than any other regiment. The Second Army, also on the Meuse-Argonne Front had over 10,000 engineers involved in road repair and construction. Taken together, these engineers made up about four percent of the combatant troops on the Meuse-Argonne Front.

During the month of October records show that 107 kilometers of roads were maintained. Dad, Dunk and their fellow engineers were obviously very busy keeping the roads passable so that army troops and artillery could continue the offensive. In the Verdun Battlefields area, as in many other parts of the Meuse-Argonne area, every inch of ground had been pounded by mortars and artillery since 1916. On the first day of the Battle of Verdun in February 1916, it is calculated that over a million shells were fired and many of the German ones weighed two tons apiece. It has also been estimated that at least one ton of ordnance was dropped on every square yard of land on the Verdun Front. To this day the shell craters are eerily visible.

Dad, meanwhile, also seems to have been busy delivering orders here and there, as his diary entries below indicate. He passed through villages only very recently liberated by the Allied forces and must have seen terrible scenes of death and destruction. As his November 7th entry indicates, hastily-made graves were everywhere.

> **November 6, 1918:** Went over to Avocourt in side car with Ruge in evening and had to change tire on way home in dark.
>
> **November 7, 1918:** Ruge and I went to Remonville in side car to take orders to Co "H". Left camp 1:30 arrived H Co. 5:30 P.M. Went thru Malancourt, Montfaucon, Cierges, Romagne, Bantheville, Aincreville, and Villers. On way home got stuck on hill between Bantheville and Cunel. Worked on machine

Shell craters in the Verdun battlefield area, 2017 (JBP)

**till 10 P.M. and then salvaged some blankets from Bantheville water station (not in use as such) and slept in hole next to Germans grave, about halfway uphill. In A.M. found some canned Willie and then by hooking trucks finally got towed home. Passed thru towns of Romagne, Cierges, Montfaucon, Cheppy, Varennes, Boureuilles, Neuvilly, Aubreville, Parois, Recicourt, Dombasle. Landed home 1:30 P.M.**

Dad refers, in his November 7th diary entry above, to "canned Willie." At first I thought that must be a slang reference to Kaiser Wilhelm of Germany, but after further research it turns out that it referred to canned corned beef, although some feared it might contain horse meat. Canned Willie was apparently a staple for AEF soldiers. This is probably why Dad was never a big fan of tins of Spam or corned beef during my childhood.

So what were meals—"rations"—for WWI soldiers like when they were away from the garrison or field kitchen? The usual daily "reserve ration," in use from 1907 to 1937, consisted of twelve ounces of fresh bacon or one pound of canned meat (usually corned beef), two eight-ounce cans of hard bread or hardtack biscuits, a packet of pre-ground coffee, a packet of sugar, and a packet of salt. There was a daily "tobacco ration" of four ounces of tobacco and ten cigarette papers for soldiers to roll their own cigarettes.

When soldiers were in the trenches and unable to cook or at risk of having the food spoiled by gas, they were supplied with daily "trench rations," only used during the war from 1914 to 1918. This ration consisted of a variety of canned meats—salmon, sardines, corned beef—and was sealed in a tin box covered with canvas. It was bulky and was a limited menu, but food was food, and under extreme conditions, this ration was better than none.

The "iron ration" or emergency ration was in use from 1907 to 1922. It consisted of three 3-ounce cakes of beef bouillon powder and cooked wheat, three one-ounce bars of sweet chocolate, and salt and pepper. It was for emergency use when a soldier couldn't be supplied with food.

Referring back to the November 7th diary entry above, what must Dad and his buddy have thought as they slept in a hole next to a German grave? Perhaps, "There but for fortune go you or I." The slaughter of mainly young men in WWI was on a scale never before seen. Of the 42 million soldiers mobilized by the Allies in the war almost 5 million were killed and almost 13 million wounded—that is over 40% killed or wounded. Figures for the Central Powers (Germany, Austria-Hungary, Turkey and Bulgaria) were nearly 23 million mobilized, over 3 million killed and 8.5 million wounded—making for 50% killed or wounded. Did the young men volunteering to fight realize what the odds were for coming out of it alive?

Luckily for the AEF, General Pershing did not agree to have them under foreign command for the most part. The AEF entered the war late and American troops really didn't start fighting in battle in substantial numbers until the summer of 1918. The Americans mobilized 4.355 million troops; some 116,000 died and about 200,000 were wounded. That was less than six percent killed or wounded. Most American soldiers were involved in the war at the Front for less than its last six months and were not fighting in trench warfare—both of these facts contributed to the relatively low casualty figures for the AEF.

Another terrible consequence of war is civilian deaths. Estimates of war-related civilian deaths among the Allies is over 3.1 million and among the Central Powers almost 3.5 million. These numbers are chilling reminders of the terrible toll that any war takes on the innocent people who have to try to live through it. In many French villages in the Verdun area there are special monuments in memory of the civilians who died—not just the soldiers.

After the St. Mihiel Offensive, Sept. 12-16, 1918, in which the AEF encountered relatively little resistance from the Germans, the final major battle of the war—the Meuse

Ruins of Consenvoye, on the Meuse River just north of Verdun, from Dad's photo album. (DMB)

Argonne Offensive—was spearheaded by the AEF with help from the French. This final push to defeat the enemy started on September 26th. It was the Germans' last stand and they resisted fiercely until the Armistice on November 11th. The majority of all American deaths in WWI occurred during this time period.

Then finally—the guns went silent. The Armistice was declared to go into effect at the eleventh hour of the eleventh day of the eleventh month of 1918. Dad, always a man of few words, simply wrote in his diary:

> **Nov 11 '18 Armistice between Germany and Allies went into effect 11 A.M. French time.**

This notation was so typical of Dad, to stipulate that it was "11 A.M. French time," which of course would have been six hours earlier on the East coast of the United States or 5:00 a.m. Thus, when most Americans woke up on November 11, 1918, World War I, then known as the Great War, had already ended.

But this was definitely not the end of Army service abroad for Dad and Dunk. They both stayed on in the Meuse Valley area around Verdun to help clear up and rebuild the infrastructure so devastated by the war. In fact, they were involved in reconstruction efforts until the beginning of June 1919—spending about as much time in France after the war ended as they had during the actual war.

> **Nov. 16. Sat.** Broke camp at Verriere Farm north Dombasle this A.M. and moved to second farm in bowl of land north of Doulcon on Meuse opposite Dun. Passed thr. Malancourt, Montfaucon, Nantillois, Brieulles, Clery-le-Petit and Doulcon. Camp is in old farm buildings which are shot up by Amer. Artillery. Jack and I pretty near froze trying to get reports out in P.M. Today was coldest day so far. The ground was frozen quite deep all day.
>
> **Nov. 17, 1918.** At 5. A.M. we went under command of 3rd Army. Rode over to Remonville and got Bacorn.
>
> **Nov. 18,** Moved from camp north of Doulcon to Consenvoye. Arrived 2 P.M. Passed thru Dun, Liny,

**Sivry. And billeted in houses which are badly shot up.**

Dad and Dunk moved camp twice in the week after the Armistice. Both times they were housed in farm buildings or houses that had been damaged by the shelling as the Americans chased the Germans north out of the Meuse Valley. The weather was getting cold, the ground was frozen, and in Dunk's letter to Eileen of November 20th, the first he had written since June that survives, he describes their living quarters. They are in the town of Consenvoye, about ten miles north of Verdun on the Meuse River. Most of the building they were living in had been destroyed. They were using the only three rooms of a big old inn that weren't missing windows, doors, and roofs.

Conditions were tough. And considering wartime and early postwar conditions, it is amazing to think that letters from America ever even made it to the addressee. Dunk, himself, wonders about this in his second sentence of the letter to Eileen. He also mentions having to sew a big letter "A" on the left shoulder of his uniform, but is not sure what it means. It happens to be a shoulder sleeve insignia indicating that he was in the First Army of the AEF. Presumably, this was a way to quickly identify soldiers in the field, and probably important in identifying First Army soldiers who had recently gone under command of the Third Army. To this day, the big "A" remains the insignia of the First Army.

On Active Service with the American

Expeditionary Force

Nov. 20, 1918

Darling Girl:-

I received your letter a couple of days ago but we have been on the move so I had no chance to answer it.

I wonder when you wrote it if you ever thot where I'd receive it. That was what I thot of when I first got it, where we were camped at an old French farm up here the other side of the German lines. We had just pulled in for the night and established an office in the loft of the big barn when the dispatch rider brough in a few letters and yours was amongst 'em. Well I sure enjoyed it and wanted to answer right away but we were too busy and cold etc. and the next day I rode 40 miles on a scouting trip for a new camp and the next day we moved 9 miles and landed here last night late and to day we've had all the teams out on a long gravel haul, and to-night I've shaved and sewed the big A on my left sholder. I don't know what it means but it had to be done and I had the duce of a time doing it because if theres any thing I don't like it's sewing.

I suppose you will think because the war is over we wont be so busy but we are just about. We work from dark to dark just the same. This part of the country is latterly busted to peaces and it seems to be up to us to fix it up before they'll bring us home, but theres a lot of us here so it should'nt take very long.

You pluckie little Dear you, your all right I guess when you can stick it out there. I aught to be able to stay with it here with out grumbling but I sure wish they'd hurry up and send us home, because I don't think I can stand it very much longer with out seeing you. Well I should say you had quite a party with your chickens. I guess I'd better get back if I did'nt get so many letters I'd be worring. As far as your cooking goes I guess its' all right. Any one with a Mother like yours, could'nt help but be able to get away with the coulenry Dept. I hope I get some of those pictures. That was the only thing I wanted to send you my Christmas box tag for, so you could send them to me, but I knew, -- well I just did'nt like to send it that way it made it look to much like I was expecting two much and I was'nt able to do my share in return.

Yes Honey I guess I'll be home for next summer all right at least it looks like it now. Our troops went in to Germany and there is hundred of French and Russian prisoners coming out now. We meet bands of them all along the roads every day. They don't look so bad either.

I wish I could get home this winter some times I almost forget what home look like and if it was'nt for you I sure would forget I ever had one. In fact if you were'nt waiting for me to come I'd not come, but with you there I can't come too soon. I often find my self wondering what kind of a world this would be for me if it were'nt for you. I guess I'd better tell you about some thing else. It would hurt like blases if I thot you doubted this, and its' hard to expess ones self in a letter.

We are camped in a big old Inn to-night in an old French town there are just three rooms in the place that are'nt shattered and we have taken them. They are pretty nice to along side of the dugouts we've had to live in. We have a fire place in one corner and it looks nice but fails to do much heating.

Well Dear I guess I'll turn in. I've got one good thing here and that is plenty of good blankets so I can keep warm at night and sleep, so don't worry about me Honey and take car of your own dear little self. But your home now are'nt you?

>Good night Little Girl

>Yours

>Dunk.

>>Sgt. G. W. Duncan
>>Wgn. Co. # 3. 23rd Engrs
>>A.E.F.

>>France

Dunk's letter mentions the large numbers of returning French and Russian prisoners held by the Germans, who were making their way home or to a place where they could get transportation home. His prediction of arriving home the next summer was completely accurate; Dad and Dunk stayed in the Verdun area for another six and a half months to participate in post-war reconstruction.

Dad and Dunk both had horses and so there were several times in November and December when Dad mentioned in his diary that he and Dunk and other fellow soldiers rode horseback out into the former "no man's land" just to the east of Consenvoye, where they were living. This area was the scene of bitter fighting in 1916 and again right at the end of the war only a few weeks before. It was not uncommon to find still unburied German soldiers, as Dad notes in his diary entry below. Sometimes they inspected German trenches or machine gun nests on the Woëvre Plain just to the east of the Heights of the Meuse where the Germans had been entrenched for some four years. At other times Dad and Dunk rode on errands to the neighboring villages. Because they were both part of a wagon company, for the most part they didn't have access to motorized transport.

> **Nov. 23, Sat. Dunk, Woods and I went for horse back ride thru hills back of Sivry and Consenvoye and N. of Etraye. Saw several Germans still unburied.**

Dunk's next letter to Eileen reiterated the theme of going home. All of the fellows spent their time talking about home and wondering when they would ever get there. Once the pressure of the war was gone, Dad and Dunk and their buddies must have just wanted to get out of France and get back to America as soon as possible. Dunk, mentions, however what a huge task it would be to repatriate all of the hundreds of thousands of soldiers in the AEF and he knew that it would be some time before they made it back. In the meantime, their superiors had them working hard on repairing the roads which had been so badly damaged during the war. Everyone had a job to do and that, at least, took their minds temporarily off the thoughts of home.

On Active Service with the American Expeditionary Force

Nov. 23, 1918

Well Dear:-

Here it is three days later and I've not had a chance to send this yet, and I suppose your watching each mail as usual even if the war is over. And I suppose you will be like we are here now ever bit of news we can get is looked over to see if it has any thing about going home if it has'nt then we don't want it. How ever you must'nt get impatient as it will be a big job to move us back and no doubt will be spring before we are moved from here. I know this does'nt sound good but we'll have to buck up and stand it I guess. We are still camped out here on "No Mans Land" fixing up the delapated roads, and thinking about what we will do when we get back to the states. It's worse now than ever, we keep each other miserable talking about the nice things we can remember.

Well Honey you're the nicest thing I can remember I can assure you, and I'm not talking but I'm thinking more than ever.

How is shool going? Fine of course but you must'nt work to hard at it Dear. I must close now and I'll try to get this off to-day.

    Yours Always

    Dunk.

        Sgt. G. W. Duncan

        Wgn. Co. # 3. 23rd Engrs

        A.E.F.

        France

---

Engineer Wagon Co. #3, 23rd. Engineers.
APO 914 Amer. E. F.   Nov. 25, 1918

From:- Sgt. Duncan 2506485 Geo. W. and Sgt. Burckett 2506468 Douglas M. of Eng. Wgn. Co. #3, 23rd. Engrs.

To:- Commanding Officer, 23rd Engrs, thru military channels.

Subject:- Leave.

1. In accordance with GO #6, GHQ. AEF. 1918 we request leave to visit Glasgow and Edinburgh, Scotland for the purposes of attending to some property matters and visiting relatives. As we are now on this side of the Atlantic Ocean this leave would be very advantageous for us both. Request that the leave take effect as soon as possible.

2. Owing to the distance and uncertainty of travel, and the time which might be necessary to transact the business, request an extension of several days on the regular seven days leave if possible.

3. Left the United States, March 30, 1918 and arrived for duty with the Amer. E. F. April 13, 1918. Neither of us have had a leave since arriving overseas.

Dad and Dunk's leave request for Scotland, Nov. 25, 1918 (JBP)

**Leave request denied by General Pershing.** (JBP)

 By the end of November 1918 both Dad and Dunk had been in the Army for at least a year with no time off. After almost four months at the Front and after some eight months in France, they decided to ask permission for leave to "…visit Glasgow and Edinburgh, Scotland for the purpose of attending to some property matters and visiting relatives." Dad's mother and both of Dunk's parents were born in Scotland and they still had family there, plus Dunk was part owner of a house in Glasgow that was being sold. Their company commander recommended that their leave be granted saying, "The records of these two men have been excellent. Neither one of them has had a leave previous to or since his arrival in the Amer. E.F." It was then approved by the commanding officer of the 23rd Engineers, by the Chief Engineer of the 1st Army, and by the Chief of Staff of the First Army. Unfortunately, when it arrived at the General Headquarters of the A.E.F. the decision was not positive: "Disapproved at this time. By command of General Pershing." Their dreamed of leave in Scotland was not to be.

 All was not doom and gloom, however, because Thanksgiving Day had come. Dunk and a friend had gone two days earlier to the city of Nancy and had brought back all kinds of goodies for the traditional Thanksgiving meal. Dad, in his diary entry below, relates what a wonderful time they all had enjoying the well-known holiday food items. I can only imagine how they miraculously prepared this very complete dinner given the conditions under which they were living. Did they hire a local cook or did they themselves share the preparation and cooking duties on what was probably fairly basic cooking equipment? In any case it was a day they all fondly remembered, including the evening when they gave hospitality to two Frenchmen who were on their way home after the war to check on their houses from which they had been evacuated.

> **Nov. 28, Thanksgiving Day. We sure had some feed. Andy Nielsen, and Dunk went to Nancy on Tuesday and brought back a lot of stuff for dinner. We had turkey, goose, mashed potatoes, turnips, dressing, gravy, apple sauce, cocoa, apple pie, chocolate iced cake, crackers, walnuts and cigarettes. We sure enjoyed it. In the P.M. a French officer and a civilian appeared upon the scene and desired shelter for the night from the rain. We fixed a bunk for them in orderly room. We found out that the officer was going to see his home in Damvillers and the civilian his home in Ecure. They seemed pretty happy and the old gent offered us a swallow of rum which the majority did not refuse. It sure seemed like a real Thanksgiving.**
>
> **Dec. 5, Rode over horse back to Damvillers, this A.M.**
>
> **Dec. 7. Dunk and I rode up to Vilosnes at night to get trans. For 2 nurses stranded in town. Got two motorcycles to take them to Souilly.**

It is certain that Dad and Dunk were working very hard on road repair, but it is equally certain that they enjoyed some off-the-road adventures. As Dad's diary entries above and below indicate, they managed to go by horseback to some of the recent battleground areas where the Germans had left some huge artillery. In the last days of the war the Germans retreated hurriedly from some sites and, of course, were unable to take all of their equipment with them. This included leaving some of the biggest guns on the field, including the German 77 field gun and a fifteen-inch gun, mentioned below, which shot shells that were fifteen inches in diameter and almost five feet long.

> **Dec. 14. Dunk, Andy and I took ride to Dannevoux. Dunk and I operated German 77 field gun. Saw big**

German artillery left in field when they retreated hastily, Dannevoux, January 1919. (DMB)

**15" gun left by Germans at Dannevoux. Projectiles 15" Diam. 4'9" long.**

Now in mid December, as the holidays approached, Dad and Dunk were given permission to take a leave. Rest and relaxation at last. It started on December 18, 1918 which was Dad's twenty-third birthday. Although the leave is referred to as a "7 days leave," this must have been in addition to the Christmas and New Year's holidays, as Dad and Dunk were actually gone for sixteen days. At least eight of those days were spent on travel to and from their destination—the French Riviera. Christmas time was, no doubt, a popular time to take days off and for most AEF soldiers probably the first time since they arrived in France that they were given permission for leave. Hence, the trains were jam packed with soldiers on leave heading to Paris and then many to the warmer south of France.

Dad's diary description below of how they actually had to use various modes of transport, including walking, and spending a night in a rest camp before they even arrived at the nearest train station in Bar-le-Duc, is quite a story. But they were young and hardy and standing up all night on the train ride into Paris and then spending the day visiting the sights of Paris before taking another night train, and sleeping in the aisle on route to the Riviera, was just part of the adventure for them. They eventually arrived in Nice, after more than four days of travel, in the middle of the night, and after finally locating a hotel, got to bed at 5:45 a.m. Today the journey from Verdun to Nice, about 550 miles, can be done in just nine hours by car.

> December 18-20, Dunk and I started on our 7 days leave to Nice. Dunk hooked ride to Verdun and I rode in side car. Had 3 chain breaks and 1 puncture. From Verdun to Rest Camp Dunk walked and I had chain trouble every once in a while. Stayed at Rest Camp over night and in morning Dec. 19 Dunk and I jumped inside car and Wilson took us to Souilly. From there we got a ride to Bar-le-Duc in YMCA. Ford. Left Bar-le-Duc at 2 AM Dec. 20 train being 3 hrs late. Had to stand up all the way into Paris arriving at 8:30 AM. Went to Am. Un. Union, Louvre, Place de la Concorde, and other points of interest.
>
> December 20-21, Left Paris at 9:00 P.M. and slept in aisle all the way to Lyon arriving at 7:15 AM 12/21/18/. Arrived at Marseilles at 3:45 PM Left 5:00 PM for Nice. Standing room only.
>
> Arrived Nice 3:15 AM Dec. 22. Finally got Hotel (New York) and got to bed at 5:45 AM. Up in time for dinner at 12:00. Went over to Casino and then walked around town in A.M. In P.M. went to Municipal Casino where there had benefit night. Sure was great. Got to bed about 2:30 AM.
>
> Dec. 23, down around Y.M.C.A. in AM. In AM. Sgt White and I walked up to Mt. Boron and Fort Mont Alban and then on up to another peak from which we could see the snow capped mountains on one side and the blue Mediterranean on the other. In P.M. over at YMCA saw show and watched dancing.
>
> Dec. 24. Went on trip to Cimiez, the residential part of Nice. An old Roman arena there. Went thru several churches and cemeteries. Bought a camera this date.

Dunk, center, and two buddies on the Promenade des Anglais, Nice, December 1918. (DMB)

Added to this entry later was "Ruth died today due to automobile accident. [6/29/19]." Ruth was Dad's only surviving sibling; the date should be 6/29/18.

Dad and Dunk had a wonderful time in the cosmopolitan city of Nice, far removed from the rigors of life and work in a devastated war zone. They and so many of their fellow soldiers richly deserved a break from the harsh conditions and hard work of AEF life both during the war and in the immediate post-war months when so much reconstruction had to be done in difficult circumstances. I can only imagine what it must have been like to sleep in a warm hotel, in a bed with sheets, and be served food in a fancy dining room. How appealing it must have been not to have to rise at 5:00 a.m. and be in bed by 10:00 p.m. Dad noted that on Christmas Eve he bought himself a camera, and with this he took many photos both while on leave and later back in the Verdun area. Dad was the photographer and so was not in most of the photos. There is a charming photo of Dunk, and another soldier buddy from the 23rd Engineers, in their uniforms sitting happily in the fancy casino dining room in Monte Carlo enjoying their meal. There is another of three

Dunk, right, and a soldier friend dining in Monte Carlo, December 1918. (DMB)

of them relaxing on a bench on the Promenade des Anglais surrounded by palm trees. How they must have reveled in the attention they received and in this life of leisure in comparison to the drudgery of their normal military life.

Dad and his friends spent a lot of time around the YMCA, including on Christmas Day, as this organization likely had lots of appealing free-of-charge activities for soldiers. The Y was a kind of home away from home for most AEF soldiers and provided free or low-cost snacks; free reading materials; and free movies, shows and occasionally dances.

Dad and his buddies also took several hikes into the interior toward the Alpes Maritimes from where they could see snow-capped peaks in one direction and the blue Mediterranean Sea in the opposite direction. They traveled to Monte Carlo and the Italian border, which figured in several of Dad's photos. Going to a casino in both Nice and in Monte Carlo must have been an exciting event for twenty-three year old Dad. I am sure that his strict Presbyterian upbringing had not included any visits to casinos in the U.S. He even mentions going to a "song service," which I assume was something offered on Sundays at the YMCA.

> **Dec. 25, Around Y.M.C.A. most of day. Sgt White and I went to Eldorado.**
>
> **Dec 26, Took walk up on mountains North of Nice. In PM over at YMCA and saw show.**
>
> **Dec. 27, Went to Monaco, Monte Carlo, Menton and Italian border.**
>
> **Dec. 28, Around YMCA most of day.**
>
> **Dec. 29, Down in Casino in AM. In P.M. walked up around Chateaux. In evening went to song service.**

After eight splendid, relaxing days by the Mediterranean, it was time for Dad, Dunk and their buddies to return to Verdun. The return train trip again took four whole days, via Marseilles, Lyon, Paris and Bar-le-Duc. They apparently had a long enough layover in Marseilles to take in a show by Gaby Deslys, a famous performer whose 1911 visit to Yale University had occasioned a student riot. Reviews of the period called her an "irresistible singer, actress, and dancer."

> **Dec. 30, Left Nice on 6:30 AM for Marseilles. Arrived there 3:30 P.M. Went to show by Gaby Deslys in P.M. Had room at Lafayette Hotel.**
>
> **Dec. 31, Walked around town. Left on 12:30 PM train for Lyon.**
>
> **January 1-2, 1919: Jan 1st Arrived Paris at 12:00 noon. Down at University Bureau for a while. Left Paris at 8 P.M. arrived Nancy 7AM Jan. 2 Left 9 AM. Arrived Bar-le-Duc 12:30 PM Jan 2.**
>
> **Jan 3, Left Bar-le-Duc. 6 AM. Arrived at Camp Consenvoye 2 P.M.**

After three more days on the train, including New Year's Eve, and with brief periods in Lyon, Paris, Nancy and Bar-le-Duc, they arrived back at their camp in Consenvoye. There they were, again living in a mostly-destroyed building, in a severely-devastated area, in the cold January weather of northeastern

*Section One, Wagon Co. #3, 23rd Engrs. leaving Consenvoye, Meuse, France, for Verdun. Meuse River in background. Jan. 7th/1919.*

From Dad's album (DMB)

France. It must have taken a bit of getting used to after their dream vacation staying in luxurious quarters in warm southern climes and being served meals by waiters, attired in crisp white shirts. However, neither Dad in his diary, nor Dunk in his letters, complained about the return to the reality of early post-WWI in the Meuse area.

### Jan. 7, Section One and Hdqs. Left Consenvoye for Verdun.

Just four days after arriving back from leave, Dad and Dunk were again on the move, this time to about ten miles south along the Meuse River to the city of Verdun. As we know from both accounts and photographs of the period, including some pictures taken by Dad, Verdun had been badly shot up by the Germans during their 1916 unsuccessful Battle of Verdun. Wagon Company #3 was housed in the French Ministry of Defense's Miribel Barracks just east of the Meuse River. The Miribel site consisted of two enormous stone buildings, each of four stories. The buildings, however, looked like skeletons of their former selves due to the intense shelling during the war. It is not clear whether Dad and Dunk camped on the grounds at Miribel or actually lived in the scarcely-inhabitable buildings. What they did enjoy later in the spring, however, in their free time, as evidenced by some of Dad's photos, is games of baseball. There is one iconic image of a guy stretching to make a catch with a skeletal barracks in the background.

Living in Verdun, in contrast to in the small village of Consenvoye, afforded Dad and Dunk an opportunity to be closer to some activities in which they could take part to try to forget about their daily routines. Dunk, by now, was

Playing baseball at Caserne Miribel, 1919. (DMB)

really getting tired of army life and wanted to get back home to Western Montana and the gal he left behind. His letter of February 2, 1919 expressed these thoughts to Eileen. In fact, Dunk had written her a very long letter but tore it up as he didn't want to really let her know how down he was feeling. In this letter below, he imagines that he is far, far away from the clean-up operations and ruins in post-war France and that he is back with her, all dressed up in his best clothes, spending a pleasant Sunday afternoon in her company. It is the kind of daydream that allows him to continue believing that he will, eventually, return to everything and everyone that he loves best. Leaving his present difficult reality, even if just for a moment, allowed him to gain the strength to continue on to the next day. As Dad's diary usually just recorded the facts, it is crucial that Dunk's letters to Eileen give us some kind of feeling of the state of these young men's minds. Dunk also mentions how eager he is to get the photos that Dad (called "B" for Burckett in the letter below) had taken of him in Nice so that he could send them to Eileen. He then goes on to say how Dad is a nice kid, but sometimes drives him crazy when he's around, not letting Dunk forget to do anything. However, Dunk admits that he really misses Dad when he's away, and also relates how much Dad looks up to him and will do whatever he asks him to do. This sounds very much like an older brother-younger brother situation to me.

Not long after returning to Verdun from his leave on the French Riviera, Dunk received a letter from one of his buddies, 2nd Lieutenant Pat Kelly, complaining how Dunk had wasted his leave by going off with Dad. Pat remarked that although Dad was a "nice kid," he was no fun. Dunk then tells Eileen about an upcoming trip he has planned to take with Lt. Pat Kelly to Paris. He mentions how expensive Paris is, and on a soldier's pay of eight dollars a month, that must have been very true. But Dunk seems desperate to get away from his current daily grind and looks forward to another adventure away from camp. By now he had been away from home for well over a year and the separation and loneliness are starting to take a toll on

Meuse River and ruins in Verdun, 1919 (DMB)

him. Having heard the news that the AEF was supposed to be disbanded in six months he waxes poetic as he describes what he plans to do when he returns. And more than anything else, he thanks Eileen for being such a wonderful letter writer; he lets her know how important her letters and her caring are to him. The last part of the letter refers to Eileen's sister Irma and how she had not been well, and how Eileen had had to take time off from school to care for her. It is possible that Irma had contracted the Spanish Flu, which raged from the spring of 1918 to early 1919. Luckily, if this were the case, she had survived. Worldwide it is estimated that at least 50 million people died due to the 1918-19 Spanish Flu.

On Active Service with the American<br>Expeditionary Force<br>2/2/19/

Eileen Dearest:-

I guess its' time I took this old stub of pencile and departed hence from these parts with you for a while sitting around here in these old tumble down buildings by ones self on a nice wintery Sunday after noon is derpressing on ones mind, if one has the mind to depress.

I got a feeling I aught to put on a clean white colar and a civilian suit and take a walk over and see you this afternoon. That is what I should be doing, but instead I have entertained a buk private a Captain, a Loot. and a Sgt. all in that order this afternoon when I felt more like being entertained by you. So as soon as they were gone I got busy and reread your last four letters which I have just reed and forthwith I burned up the longest letter I ever wrote you, and desided to start all over, so for that very good reason I haven't sent you out a letter for three or four days, because I wrote some thing I did'nt like in the first place, and then because on Jan. 6th you wrote to me and I guess were in a very good mood when you dit it so you changed things all around and now I'm going to try to write a nice agreeable letter how ever I don't know how nice and agreeable it will be as I'm being acused of of being a crank on all sides. But with all that I notice they all seem to like me pretty good, and Lt. Pat Kelly has written two letters in one week trying to arrange it so I'll meet him in the near future for a little trip, so I have made up my minde that we're going to visit Paris for three day beginning Feb. 25th. Pat may change it to some other date but I'm pretty sure we'll make it before long. Paris is expencive as the duce but Gee Whize if I could'nt go there or some place away from here once in a while I'd go crazy honey crazy as a loon this place is awful, all the pleasure there is here is sleep and get a letter from you once in a while. I don't like to kick like this but I must have some excuse for writing such bum letters get me. Oh yes I got some pictures coming B. took down at Nice I'm ancious to see 'em. I'll send 'em to you when I get to look 'em over if he hasn't beat me to it. That kid hes the bane of me life when I'm around him I do nothing but cuss him and when I'm away from him I miss him, and he'll do any thing for me wheather I want it or not. Theres no chance of me forgetting any thing when he's around. He'll make me remember it wheather I want to or not.

It is nice of you dearie to remember that suite I got I'd almost forgotten it my self I got it in the summer you know, and its' light waight. I put the coat on once at the tailor shop and its' fine fits beautiful infact its' to fine for a Sgt. To ware over here so I turned it over to Archie B. to put away for me and I haven't seen it since he's got it some place. I guess I'll ware it when I come home next winter or summer or when ever we do come. I see by the paper the A.E.F. is to be mustered out in six months I hope its' the truth if it is we aught to get home some time in July. So don't you even think of stoping writing, because I'm going to need those blessed letters of yours for a long time yet even after I get back in the states I expect, so if your pen is beginning to get a little lazy you just shake it up and keep it going. I know it is'nt though dearest you're the best girl in the world and I know it! I watch the dates on every leter you write and don't you ever think I don't appreciate all those late hours you put in writing to me after every one else is in bed, because I do. I think about you every night sitting up there writing to me, and I know just how hard it is and cold and every thing else about it. And I'm the proudest man in the regiment over all the letters I receive from you, and I'm not the only one notices it they all do and they kid me about the purpal ink but it does'nt hurt my feeling a bit believe me I like it.

Say you aught to see Kellys last letter that girl of his Blanche by name it seems is well again and he's going home and get married right off, and he's Montana struck and he's coming out west with her so she'll be sure to keep that said health of hers. I hope he can land a job in Msla. If he does we'll have some might good interesting neighbors. It's to bad he had to leave Rochester N.Y. He's got a big job there asst. City Engr. But he's coming west sure I guess. He'll be some one for you to argue with, and he's some good little poker player to by the way, if he can get in and started I think he'll be quiet an asset to the crowd. He's an interesting talker, and likes to. I guess thats why he enjoys me I let him do the talking.

I wonder why you layed so much stress on the overcoat you wished me to ware. I don't ware one atall we all ware Mackanows. I never did have an over coast, and when I get back to dear old Missou I hope I wont need one believe me. I'm looking forward to droping in there some nice hot day next summer, when straw hats and ice cream are invogue. Ice cream Gee Whize! I have'nt seen ice cream since I left Spokane. What do you think of that. I'd like to get back just about straw berry time. I don't believe I've had any thing good to eat for years. Honest you can't get any thing real good over here like Mother or Mrs. C. cooks, with all the French bragging about good food. I'd give just any thing for one good cup of coffee.

I just don't know where you get the idea theres so many things these days to make one forget. I'm sure theres nothing on this end. It must be with you. I couldn't forget any thing if I wanted to I can remember every little thing you ever did or said, and I think of them so much I think I'm going "bugs". Nope my dear there is'nt any one forgetting the least little thing on this end. I'd write every day if I could send them but I can't send 'em out only once in a while and if they lay around I read 'em over and then burn them up because I think of something else. I'm mighty glad Irma is coming along fine and is out again, and that you can go back to school. I'll bet Mother is relieved.

    Good night Dear I must close

        Always Yours

           "Dunk"

                Sgt. G. W. Duncan

                Wgn. Co. # 3. 23rd Engrs

                A.E.F. France

The winter of 1919 was bitterly cold and for much of February there was snow on the ground in Verdun. Dad's photos of his buddies, of German prisoners at the Verdun railway station, and his picture of Wagon Company #3's eight-horse wagon at Souilly all show that snow. Souilly was the town about ten miles southwest of Verdun where General Pershing had the headquarters of the AEF during the Meuse-Argonne Offensive. Field Marshall Petain had also had his headquarters there during the 1916 Battle of Verdun. There was a competition in Souilly in February 1919 among wagons pulled by eight

Cpl. Baron + Wag. Dick and "eight up" which took 1st prize at Horse Show at Souilly. Verdun. Feb. 1919.

**From Dad's album (DMB)**

horses. Dad seemed proud that their wagon from Wagon Company #3 had won the meet.

Now that Dad was in Verdun, it seems that his services as an electrical engineering student were put to good use. He and his buddy Hamer got the YMCA theater all renovated with new wiring. They even went to a dance there and mentioned the existence of some ladies, so life couldn't have been too terrible. From time to time they even went by truck with some of their "gang" to see shows in the nearby village of Billy.

**Feb. 15.** Went to Souilly to Wgn. Train Horse Show. Wgn.#3. Won meet.

**Feb. 23- Mar. 1st** Hamer and I wired theater in Verdun for Y.M.C.A.

**March 7, 1919:** Hamer and I went to dance at theater. After dance went up to Miss Sheerer's and Miss Guy's room and we had a little party in honor of Hamer's going away to school at AEF University at Beaune, Cote d'Or. Got home about 1:00 A.M.

**March 8, 1919:** Hamer and other fellows left for school.

The AEF University, located just to the south of Dijon in the city of Beaune, in a former 20,000 bed U.S. hospital, was organized in February 1919 to enable some 9,500 U.S. soldiers to study before they returned to the U.S. It was in operation until June 1919 and, overseen by the YMCA, some 600 teachers from the U.S. were hired to teach the troops. Men could choose from one of thirteen departments: agriculture, letters, fine and applied arts, education, journalism, correspondence, music, engineering, business administration, law, medicine, science, and citizenship. Prior to the opening of the AEF University,

Truck with soldiers from Wagon Company #3 going to a show at another company, 1919. (DMB)

hundreds of U.S. troops had been given the opportunity to study in universities in Britain and France, but due to the huge demand, the U.S. decided to open its own university in France during the immediate post-war period.

Dad and Dunk, meanwhile, have now been living in Verdun for over two months, and Dad certainly was enjoying the advantages of having a YMCA close at hand. He also enjoyed taking photos with the camera he bought in Nice, and has left a fine photographic record of many important sites in Verdun, including the Porte Chaussée entry gate to the city, the Pont Ecluse (Locks Bridge), the cathedral and College of St. Mary, the Meuse River with the ruins of buildings along the sides, and the Miribel Barracks. He also roamed further afield and took photos of several forts east of the city and also of German trenches and German artillery left in the battlefield. He has many wonderful photos of his soldier friends, often doing

Dunk in German trench on the Woëvre Plain east of Verdun, 1919. (DMB)

Dad in Haudainville, 1919 (DMB)

Dunk in Haudainville, 1919 (DMB)

silly things like pretending they are German by wearing the German spiked helmet topped off with a white plume.

But now much of Dad's company was on the move again to Haudainville, a town just three miles south of Verdun also on the Meuse River. Finally, the men seemed to have excellent quarters. Dad and Dunk must have been very busy, because although there are photos of both of them from Haudainville, Dad does not have another diary entry from his two months there and we have no surviving letters from Dunk to Eileen.

> **March 16 Sunday. Sec. #1 and Hqs of Company moved fr. Verdun to Haudainville. We sure have fine quarters. Big bed and regular furniture.**

The journey back to the U.S. began in mid May when Wagon Company #3 moved to Souilly. From there they entrained for Le Mans in central France and their train, as Dad notes in his diary, used the "Nevers cut off, which had been constructed by the 23rd engineers."

As mentioned previously, Dad and Dunk had worked for most of the four months they were stationed in Nevers, in central France, on the Nevers Cut-Off. This important railroad project, only used for three weeks before the Armistice, was

Bob Agar and his dog on train on route to Brest, May 1919. (DMB)

even more useful to the AEF when it served to bring troops quickly back from the Front to the Atlantic ports after the war. Records show that between November 11, 1918 and August 12, 1919 some 735 trains used the cut-off and carried some 735,000 men—more than one-third of all American troops in France at the time of the Armistice.

After bypassing Nevers, Dad's train stopped in Le Mans to discharge some troops. Dad spent five very busy days in Le Mans, finishing whatever paperwork he still had to complete, in his capacity as company clerk for Wagon Company #3, before entraining for Brest.

> **May 12, 1919: Whole company moved to Souilly, Meuse, at noon.**
>
> **May 15 Thursday. Entrained at Souilly, Meuse, for le Mans. Left at 10:00 A.M. passed thru St. Mihiel, Commercy, Neufchateau, Dijon, Beaune, Le Cascaux, Nevers cut off, which had been constructed by 23rd engineers, Bourges, Gievres, Tours, and then Le Mans. Arrived Saturday May 17 at 8:30 A.M.**
>
> **May 21 Wed. Left Le Mans 8:30 P.M. after working day and night to get final paper work in shape. Arrived Brest, Finistere 4 P M. May 22, Thursday.**

Dad and Dunk returned to the Pontanezen Barracks in Brest, where they had first arrived over fourteen months before. This time there were some 75,000 men billeted there. The AEF was making a huge effort to repatriate the troops as quickly as possible, so troop trains arrived in Brest daily from the Front and transports were leaving almost daily for the U.S. During the spring and early summer months of 1919 there were some 150,000 soldiers a month embarking in Brest for the U.S. and in July 1919 this figure reached a peak of 170,000. And it was not just soldiers who were returning. At the end of the war about 1,700 French war brides, some with children, were permitted to board transports for the U.S. Other records show that from May to December 1919 some 2,293 women and 200 children set sail from Brest for the U.S.—from some twenty-one nationalities, but mostly French.

Tents at Pontanezen with duckboards neatly arranged so that soldiers could stay out of the mud. (CdI)

Dad and Dunk had to wait ten days before they embarked on the *U.S.S. Finisterre* which would take them home across the Atlantic. They would have enjoyed their last week in Brest, knowing that soon they would be homeward bound. They probably got to read a couple of editions of the famous *Pontanezen Duckboard*—a "duckboard" being the name of the wooden sidewalk boards that extended many miles throughout the camp to cover up the muddy ground, and the name given to the newspaper published by AEF soldiers at the camp. It was published twice a week from March 1, 1919 to August 2, 1919 (46 issues) and was printed at the offices of *La Dépêche*, the Brest newspaper. It contained factual articles about the AEF and events in both France and the U.S., as well as humorous articles about the soldiers' life and cartoons about the war and its aftermath.

Dunk's last note to Eileen from France was a postcard from Brest, apparently given to him by a French shopkeeper,

The *Pontanezen Duckboard* newspaper produced by the soldiers in Camp Pontanezen, June 28, 1919.

whom Dunk refers to as a "frog," a common expression used by English speakers to refer to the French. Dunk notes how much Brest had changed from just over a year ago when he arrived there. It was now practically an American city, where U.S. dollars were just as acceptable as French francs, and where "every one talks Amex." The port of Brest had been turned into a port of international importance due to its use and upgrading of facilities by the American Expeditionary Forces during WWI. Dunk was also impressed by the huge numbers of ships everywhere. And one of those ships, the U.S.S. Cap Finisterre, would soon be taking Dad and Dunk home across the Atlantic.

> Brest, France
>
> Spring 1919 on way back to U.S.
>
> When I was shoping to-day the old "Frog" that waited on me gave me this and a match box and a little dutch helmet. I think he must have been drunk. I was almost afraid to take them when he handed them out. But Brest sure has changed you would hardly know it now. They use American money just like they do their own and the Americans have got the port so its' almost clean, and every one talks Amex. There are 75000 Americans there. And ships ships ships in port, it's a great sight.
>
> D

As they left the Pontanezen Barracks and made their way down the hill to the port in Brest and the awaiting transports, what were Dad and Dunk thinking? Did they remember the excitement they had felt fourteen months earlier when they first arrived in France and marched up the hill to unknown territory? As sergeants now, both Dad and Dunk might have ridden in trucks from the camp to the port. French children might have given them flowers as they rode by, expressing the thanks of the French people to the soldiers of the AEF who had given so much to help the Allies win the war and save them from German domination.

From Dad's album, June 1919 (DMB)

USS Finisterre entering New York Harbor, June 11, 1919. (DMB)

# Chapter 7: The Return to College and Work

The journey home across the Atlantic, now free from German U-boats, took only ten days. Dad and Dunk had been away from the United States for nearly fifteen months. Everyone rejoiced as they entered New York Harbor. Dad has several photos of all hands on deck as they passed by the Statue of Liberty and headed toward the docks in Hoboken, New Jersey, from whence they came. We have no letters from Dunk to record his emotions upon landing, and Dad's diary entries are, as usual, just very factual. They still had to be discharged from service. But how joyful they must have felt to be home at last.

> **May 31, 1919: Saturday. Left Pontanezen Bks 12:00 noon and embarked on U.S.S. Cap Finisterre at 3:00 PM.**
>
> **June 1st Left France 9 AM.**
>
> **June 11, 1919: Landed at Hoboken 2:00 P.M. Took boat to Queens and train to Camp Mills, Garden City, Long Island, arriving camp 6.00 P.M.**

Returning soldiers enjoy apple pie in Hoboken, 1919. (Hoboken Museum)

> **Left Camp Mills 9. AM June 17. Arrived Camp Upton, 11:30 A.M. same date. Wgn. Co #3, passed out of service June 17, 1919.**
>
> **Left Camp Upton June 23rd and arrived Camp Dix, N.J. same date.**
>
> **Discharged from service June, 25th 1919. Arrived in Phila Pa 6/25/19. Stayed with Bill at Palmyra till 6/26/19.**

Dad had to pass through three camps—Camp Mills and Camp Upton in New York, and Camp Dix in New Jersey—over fifteen more days before he was finally "discharged from service June, 25th 1919." His Wagon Company #3 had been disbanded on June 17th, but it took another week for Dad to be freed from the military. He had no immediate family close by Camp Dix and so stayed with a relative, Bill, in a Philadelphia suburb that first night.

As a twenty-three year old returning from the Great War, what did Dad tell Bill about his experiences? What aspects of his wartime service were most important to him and what did he want to share? Conversely, what did he not want to talk about? It is often difficult to recount events to those who have not been through them. This is particularly true in the case of war, when soldiers have seen unspeakable horrors. I don't remember Dad ever speaking of any negative experiences he had during the war, but of course I was born nearly thirty years after that war ended, and by then World War II was the talk of the day. The "Great War" and its actors had faded into the past.

> **Went to Washington, D.C. 6/27/19. Returned to New York, 6/28/19. Sunday 6/29, called on M.F. Mc C in Somerville, N.J. in P.M.**

Dad spent some of the summer of 1919 visiting friends, including young lady friends, in New Jersey and Washington, D.C. He also went back to his family's farm in Somerville, New Jersey for a while, probably to help out with farm chores. While there he visited old high school friends as well as his former high school. He also had the foresight to go to nearby Morristown and take and pass the driver's test for motor

"Burcranette," Dad's family home in Somerville, New Jersey. (DMB)

vehicles. Then he headed back to Boston to return for his junior year at MIT.

Dunk, meanwhile, after being discharged took the first train out to Missoula, Montana—arriving there three days later. One can only imagine the joyous reunion of Dunk with Eileen and her family—"Mother" and sister Irma—that Dunk so often mentioned in his letters from France. He was back home, where he'd dreamed about being every night that he was in France. Life was sweet again in God's country in Western Montana.

How did Dad and Dunk re-adapt to their former lives after being away in a war zone for over a year? How did the U.S. government support them as they eased back into civilian life? Both had attained the rank of sergeant, but this didn't count for much in those days. During the war their pay was about $8.00 per month. They received virtually nothing except a $60 bonus when discharged. In May 1924 the World War Adjustment Compensation Act promised them $1 per day for service in the U.S. and $1.25 per day for service abroad up to a total of $500 and $625 respectively, but disbursed over a period of twenty years. This deferred compensation was not enough to really pay for much of anything. There were few veteran's benefits or services for those who had just returned from a war, other than a very minimal health insurance for service personnel and

Dad (front left) on the steps of MIT, with classmates, May 1917. (JBP)

vocational training for those who had been disabled. Unlike the year-long unemployment benefits given to WWII veterans, there was no unemployment assistance after WWI. AEF soldiers had to rely on charity. There were no psychologists to talk to about the terrible things they had seen in the war and for many, the terrible nightmares they must have had. After WWI it was called "shell shock"; today we know it as PTSD; post traumatic stress disorder.

On October 1, 1919 Dad left his home in New Jersey, spent the night with friends in Hartford, and on October 2nd returned to Cambridge, Massachusetts to prepare to return to his third year at MIT. It was a very, very hard time for him. He once told me that it was the most difficult year in his life. He had received almost no financial support from the army. His father gave him nothing, having recently remarried to a widow with four children of her own. It is not clear whether any of his relationships with girlfriends had survived during the time he was away in the war. It is also not clear how much he had been psychologically affected by the war and what he had seen. He had lost his beloved mother and both of his dear siblings over the past decade. His already emotionally distant father was not really able to relate to his son and his needs. But nevertheless, father and son did write often to each other. None of these letters remains, so we have no idea what they contained, but there was some kind of a relationship that Dad kept with his only living family member.

Now, back in Cambridge, Dad had to find a place to live with minimum rent and then find a job that he could do during the hours when he wasn't in class. He spent his first night in the Hotel Oxford, and then took a room on Broadway Street for a week until he found permanent housing. In less than two weeks he had secured a job with the Old Colony Ice Cream Company. He was to do the early morning ice cream truck deliveries to businesses, including MIT, in the area. He had to rise at 5:15 a.m. in order to get to work by 6:00 a.m. He drove a Ford truck. After his deliveries were finished by mid-morning, he was off to classes at MIT. It was a punishing schedule and on December 12th with a covering of snow and ice on the roads, he had a "smash up" on Charles River Road due to the slippery road surface. In his diary there is a detailed sketch of the two vehicles involved with their license plates and the directions in which they were traveling. No more information is given, so I have no idea whether he missed classes that day, had to go to court, or was assessed a fine.

Apparently the ice cream company didn't blame him as he continued working for them for the rest of the school year. And on December 23rd he arose at 4:50 a.m. and took care of the ice cream orders so that he could catch the 8:30 a.m. train for New York and then on to Somerville, New Jersey for Christmas. His one diary entry for the Christmas holidays indicated that he received a book from Miriam Frances McConaughy, one of his Somerville High School lady friends. His comment was "sure appreciate it." This was someone who had written to him and to whom he had written during the war, according to the notes in his diary. Was this a special lady friend or just one of his high school classmates? Unfortunately, we will never know.

On fall and spring weekends, when he had free time, Dad continued hiking all over the local countryside. One day he walked out to Waltham and back—about fifteen miles. Another time he and a Canadian classmate walked over to the Arnold Arboretum in the southern part of Boston, and yet another out to the Blue Hills and Braintree. He met lady friends occasionally in Cambridge and Boston, and sometimes even went out to Wellesley College to call on friends that he knew there. He mentions taking one of these ladies to the "Tech Show" at MIT and then out to dinner.

When he returned to MIT for the next semester the President, Richard Cockburn Maclaurin, had just died. Dad had noted in his diary while he was in France that President Maclaurin had written him a letter. Dad attended his funeral service on January 18th at the New Old South Church in Copley Square. It is quite a coincidence that over thirty years later Dad built our family home in a Boston suburb just across the street from President Maclaurin's younger son. I grew up playing with several of his grandchildren.

It seems that part of Dad's MIT education included visiting local businesses and utility companies, presumably to give the students a practical look at what they were studying. In his diary below he notes some of these off-site visits.

> **Wednesday. March 10th Attended lecture and pictures on Hog Island Ship Yard by Matthew C. Brush '01 in evening. In the afternoon went on trip thru "L" St. Station of Boston Edison Co.**

> **Wed. Mar. 17. '20. Visited Watter M Lowney Co. Boston, and studied welfare and employment depts.**

Dad mentioned several times during his first year back at MIT that he attended activities run by the First Baptist Church in Boston. The church was probably trying to encourage young folks to attend it and provided them with free or low cost activities to attract their interest. I imagine that it was a welcome social outlet for a student who had no family and few friends in the Boston area. Dad noted in his diary entries in later years at MIT that he was in charge of the candy, the drinks, or the "eats" for these social gatherings.

> Thursday. April 22nd. Attended Country Circus at First Baptist Church Boston. Had charge of a couple of games.
>
> Monday May 31st 1920. Mac Perkins with three girls and myself went on picnic with Baptist church to Houghtons Pond
>
> Thursday P.M. May 27, 1920. Attended annual banquet of M.I.T. branch of A.I.E.E. at Copley Sq. Hotel Boston. The speaker of evening was Elihu Thomson.

Dad was a lifelong member of the American Institute of Electrical Engineering (AIEE), later the IEEE, and notes in his diary indicate that he went to meetings of its MIT branch. On one particular night the speaker was Elihu Thomson, an early pioneer of DC and AC power, a lecturer for over forty years at MIT, and its acting president from March 1920 to July 1921 and again from November 1921 to January 1923. His Thomson-Houston Company merged with the Edison Company to form General Electric. He was also a former president of the AIEE. As an electrical engineering student, it is very likely that Dad had Elihu Thomson, one of the most influential individuals in electrical engineering but also one of the least well-known, as one of his professors. Other AIEE meetings that Dad attended had speakers on radio telephony and on the history of the telephone.

During his first year back at MIT Dad had written at least eight times to Dunk in Missoula, Montana. Dunk had written almost the same number of letters back to Dad. This was also true during the second year back and only slightly fewer letters were written the third year after the war. This is what I can glean from Dad's letter writing records. What I can imagine is that Dad was eager to go visit Dunk in Montana, but had neither the financial means nor the time to do so. But it was always in the back of his mind, and I'm sure Dunk encouraged Dad to keep thinking about it.

As the 1919-20 school year came to an end, Dad was eager to stop his hard life of getting up early to work and then going to class all day. He notes in his diary that June 6, 1920 was his last day employed by the Old Colony Ice Cream Co. And then he left two days later for home in Somerville, New Jersey for a few days. Next he was off to Washington, D.C. for a few days to see a lady friend and arrange his forward travel for his summer job at Ft. Monroe, Virginia.

> **Sunday June 6th Last day of work for Old Colony Ice Cream Co.**
>
> **June 8. Tues. Went home, arriving 1 AM. June. 9.**
>
> **June 13, Sunday. Motored to Phila. and stayed overnight with Bill at Palmyra N.J.**
>
> **Monday. June 14. Left Phila. and arrived Washington 5. PM. Stayed St. James hotel.**
>
> **Tues. June 15th. After getting transportation fixed up at Zone transportation office, I met Miriam at noon time at the Washington Hotel and we had lunch together. In the evening Miriam and I had dinner and then we went out to her domicile and I met Estelle. In the evening we all went to the Belasco theatre and saw 'A Thief for a Night' written by May Robert Reinhart.**
>
> **Wed. June 16. Miriam and I had lunch together. Also saw her for a few moments before leaving to take boat to Fort Monroe. My stay was certainly very pleasant and Miriam was very enjoyable. Left at 6.30 PM on S.S. Southland on N & W SS. Co. for Fort Monroe.**
>
> **June 17. Thursday. Arrived Fort Monroe for 6 wks camp work on Coast Artillery @ 6:30AM. Assigned Bat. "A".**

Fort Monroe, Virginia, where Dad spent six weeks of "camp work" on Battery "A" of the Coast Artillery was a fort that had been built from 1819-34 on a strategic site at the end of a narrow strip of land jutting out from the Newport News-Hampton, Virginia peninsula at the southwest entrance to Chesapeake Bay. The fort was named after President James Monroe and was a Union stronghold throughout the Civil War.

The Coast Artillery was in need of electrical work and Dad and his coworkers, mainly other engineering students, were tasked with making the necessary repairs. Today it would be less than a four-hour car drive from D.C. to Ft. Monroe, but in the early 1900s the easiest, and probably most economical, way to get there apparently, was by boat from Washington, D.C. — a trip that took about twelve hours.

The work on the electrical systems of the coast battery was a way that Dad could put what he had learned in class at MIT into practice in a real setting. He was appointed Battery Commander and the six weeks he spent there, mostly with other men his age, would have been a welcome respite from the drudgery of life in Cambridge during the school year. As his diary indicates he was able to take off on long weekends to visit his lady friend in D.C. On other weekends he visited Knox relatives, from his mother's family, in Norfolk. He also took advantage of free time to visit the ship yards in Newport News, the Naval Base in Norfolk and the town and battlefield of Yorktown. He and some of his work camp colleagues even spent five days working at Camp Eustis. This camp, which had been established as a coast artillery replacement center for Fort Monroe and a balloon observation school, was along the James River.

> **June 26, 1920: Nesmith, Blerrer and I called on Harry Field at Norfolk in AM. In morning I went thru ship yards at Newport News.**
>
> **July 3rd Sat. Crawford and I went to Washington, D.C. via Richmond, leaving Ft. Monroe 12:45PM. Arriving W.@ 6:45PM. Had supper with M.F.McC and then we went to Keiths.(In margin is written "Went to Langley Field in A.M.")**
>
> **Monday July 5, M.F.McC and I went horse back riding thru Rock Creek Park in A.M. We had dinner together. Left on 6.30 PM boat with Crawford for Ft. Monroe.**
>
> **July 6. Tuesday. Arrived O.K. at Ft. Monroe. 7.00 AM.**

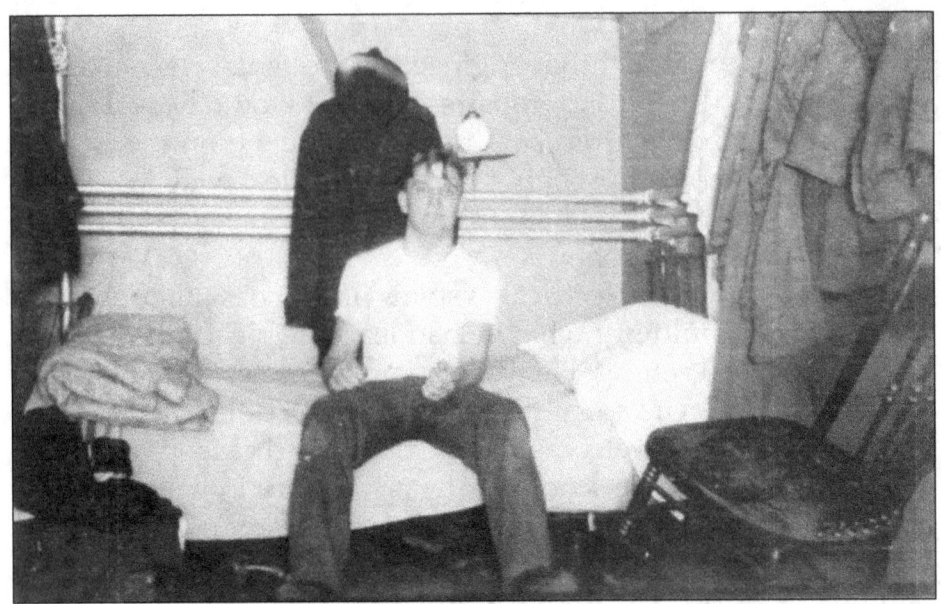

MIT classmate at Dad's bedroom on Beacon Street, Boston, 1920-22. (DMB)

**July 10, 1920: Sat. Went to Naval Operating Base in AM. Called on Walter Knox and family at Norfolk in A.N.**

**July 12. Monday. Moved from Ft. Monroe @ 8.30 AM and arrived @ Camp Eustis at 11.15 AM, which is near Lee Hall, Virginia.**

**Wed July 14, 1920. Crawford and I went to Yorktown in P.M. Rather quaint and a fine view from monument across river York.**

**Sat. July 17, Broke Camp at Eustis and returned to Ft. Monroe. Time of travel 2 h 40 min by truck thru Newport News and Hampton.**

After the six week work camp at Fort Monroe, Dad returned for a visit to his home in Somerville, New Jersey, before heading to MIT for his senior year at the beginning of October 1920. He initially rented a room in Cambridge and went back to working at the Old Colony Ice Cream Company, making deliveries from 4:30 - 8:30 a.m. Mondays through Saturdays and every other Sunday. For this he was paid $15 a week. After about a month of this exhausting schedule, he quit. On November 4th

Dad's study on Beacon Street, Boston, 1920-22. (DMB)

he moved to a building on Beacon Street in Boston where he received room, board and a small monthly sum for "taking care of furnace and other small jobs." It must have been a great relief for Dad to know that he didn't have to wake up in the middle of the night almost daily and then go to classes where he had to concentrate on the technical aspects of electrical engineering. He could now lead a more typical student life, although I'm sure he had to spend many evenings shoveling coal into the furnace and doing other janitorial type jobs. He kept this job until June 1922, and on at least one occasion noted in his diary he had to stay up all night fixing a broken furnace and replacing the needed parts.

Dad spent much of the final semester of his senior year, including the following summer, doing research for his thesis at a hydroelectric station in Concord, New Hampshire. On many occasions he had to commute to Concord and return the same day so as to be able to fulfill his duties as building janitor where he lived. Disaster struck in March 1921 when in just three days' time his father died in a New York hospital. Dad missed seeing him alive by less than three hours. It was doubly hard, then, when only a few months later Miriam Frances, one of his dearest Somerville High School lady friends, died suddenly.

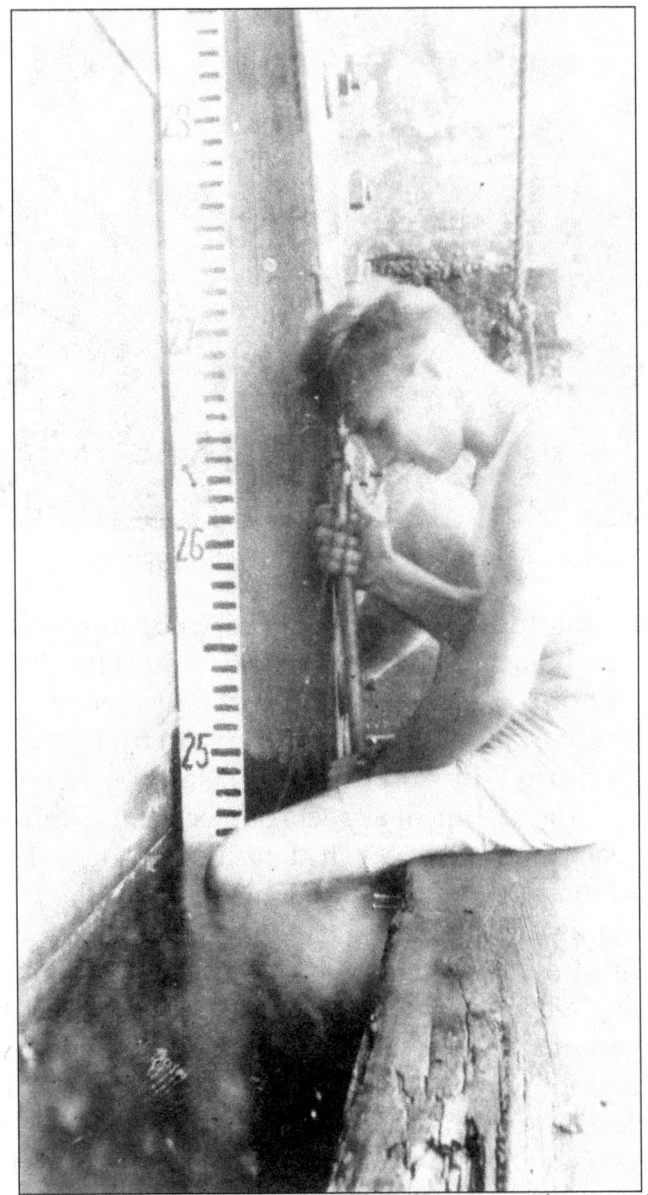

Dad measuring tailwater at Sewall's Falls Power Plant on the Merrimack River, Concord, New Hampshire, July 1921. (DMB)

These months were very dark ones for Dad and that is probably why he didn't finish his senior thesis until the fall of 1921.

In November 1921 he presented his thesis titled "Efficiency test on the triplex turbine and direct connected generator of

Concord Electric Company's hydro-electric station at Sewall's Falls, New Hampshire." By then he had already decided to stay at MIT another year for graduate work in electrical engineering.

He spent much of this final year, 1921-22, on a project surveying the land and assessing the hydrology of the future Quabbin Reservoir area in central Massachusetts. He presented his master's thesis on "An investigation of the hydrology of the Swift, Ware, and Quaboag Rivers in Massachusetts" and in June 1922 received both a BS and MS in electrical engineering. Unfortunately, his father did not see his son reach this milestone. His stepmother, however, did come up from New Jersey for the commencement ceremonies. Dad was always considered to be of the Class of 1919, even though he didn't graduate until 1922, as he had started his MIT studies in 1915, and should have finished his BS in 1919, but didn't due to his service in WWI.

Meanwhile, what was Dunk doing out in Missoula after his discharge from the AEF? In late June 1919, upon parting ways with the army, he had taken the first train he could get out to Montana from the East Coast, arriving there three days later. I can only imagine the wonderful welcome he received from Eileen and her family. "Mother" probably cooked him the best meal he'd eaten since he'd left Missoula. Eileen and Dunk hadn't seen each other in just over eighteen months, and when you are young and in love that is one heck of a long time, so I'm sure they made up for lost time. Dunk got to take Eileen out in the car in the beautiful mountain scenery. They got to go out dancing and partying. They also got to play cards with their usual bunch. They got to relax and bring each other up to date on everything that had happened since they'd last seen each other.

Dunk then went back to work as a road engineer for the U.S. Forest Service (USFS) out of their Missoula headquarters. As most of the work was opening up the wilderness for the burgeoning timber industry, he was usually working offsite in far western Montana and northern Idaho. He had asked for Eileen's hand in marriage, and so about a year after returning

Dunk, Eileen, and Dad, USFS Camp 1, Kaniksu National Forest, near Priest River, Idaho, 1922. (DMB)

from the war, he and Eileen were married in Missoula in October 1920. Dunk was thirty-two years old and Eileen was only twenty-two. She had just graduated with a bachelor's degree in English from the University of Montana that June. She was quite the social butterfly and the wedding was a grand affair. They made a lovely couple and enjoyed many activities in common. They both enjoyed riding horses, hunting small animals and birds with shotguns, spending evenings socializing and playing cards with their friends, and taking rides in the car

Dad and Eileen Duncan (center two) on kitchen duty, Camp 1, 1922. (DMB)

out in the countryside. Dunk enjoyed tinkering with anything mechanical and Eileen enjoyed writing poetry.

As a married couple they moved to a Forest Service camp near Priest River, Idaho—a small, but growing town that was the center of the timber industry. Eileen managed to get hired as an accountant for the USFS. At this time Priest River was a thriving community with a population many times larger than what it is today. It was the center of the Idaho timber industry and had theaters, many stores and saloons as well as, most likely, brothels.

Meanwhile, back on the East Coast in June 1922, after graduating from MIT, Dad decided to seek his fortune and a job out in Missoula, Montana. Dunk had talked to him a lot during the war years about Western Montana and the pioneering spirit and the job opportunities out there. They had been in contact via letters on almost a monthly basis during the years Dad was finishing his studies at MIT. Now Dad was ready for a new challenge, a cross-country adventure, and needed a job. He was convinced, perhaps by Dunk, that he had the skills that the United States Forest Service (USFS) was seeking. He looked forward to seeing his best wartime buddy again and also to meeting the enchanting Eileen. So on June 14, 1922 he set off hitchhiking across the country to Missoula, Montana and then on to Priest River, Idaho where Dunk and Eileen were living and working. The journey, via Denver, and visiting friends, former classmates, and a couple of 23rd Engineers along the way, took just over two months.

Dad arrived in Priest River on August 19th and almost immediately found himself a job as a surveyor with the USFS. He spent the better part of the next three years working as a surveyor, a truck driver, a project supervisor, and then as a power plant engineer in the Priest River, Idaho and the Eastern Washington state area for the Forest Service and the Washington Water Power Company. He was of course thrilled to meet Eileen and to be close to Dunk. I'm sure that at this point Dad considered them the family that he no longer had. They lived as neighbors in one of the USFS camps (Camp #1, Lower West Branch in Kaniksu National Forest) in the Priest River, Idaho area. There are several photos of Dunk, Dad, and Eileen in camp by their tents as well as a photo of Dad, with a cook's apron on, with Eileen next to him when they were on kitchen duty in from of the cook tent. Life was pretty basic, but no worse than what Dad and Dunk had endured in France during the war. In the winter it seems that they all moved into town to Priest River and lived in log cabins.

After working as a surveyor for his first nine months out west, Dad was then employed for the spring of 1923 helping to establish a power plant at Kettle Falls on the Columbia River for the Washington Water Power Company. The work he had done for his bachelor's thesis at MIT on a power plant in New Hampshire, I'm sure, served him well on this project. He then worked again for the same company on the hydroelectric power plant at Long Lake in Washington from August 1923 to January 1924. Between these jobs he was back again in the Priest River area—photos of him, Eileen, and Dunk from this time appear in his albums. Soon, however, in March 1924 Dunk and Eileen's daughter Margaret was born and they moved to a house in town. It seems that at this point Dad left Idaho to work for a year for the Great Northern Railway in Vancouver, British Columbia. Was this interest in railroads a carryover from his WWI days working on the Nevers Cut-Off in France? That is an interesting question, but in any case he used his engineering skills to help build and electrify some new piers that the Great Northern was building along the shore in Vancouver.

But by the summer of 1925 Dad was back in Priest River working for the USFS as a truck driver. He ferried supplies between this town and the camps. He also made many trips to Spokane, Washington—about a four hour drive away—often to bring fire equipment there and buy food to bring home. In his "Field Diary and Travel Record" for July 1925, for example, Dad writes of taking seed extract and plant materials to the camps, as well as oats, hay (presumably for the horses and mules that were still used in logging operations), and culvert pipe (for the roads). Additionally, this diary mentions taking supplies to several area fires, including "rations for the fire crew." Dad also worked as some sort of supervisor, because in his August 1925 diary he wrote:

> **Left Priest River 8:30AM. Arr. Bonners Ferry 12:30PM. Arr. Camp Skin Creek 2 PM. Went over work project cleared of brush and timber. Stumps blown from Sta. 32-38 to end of project. Small stumps not pulled yet.**

This same month he refers to work he did on two fire lookouts—North Baldy (6,300 feet elevation) and Monumental (5,700 feet). He notes that he took a "pack horse"(for carrying supplies) and a "saddle horse" (for himself) and put fifty-four insulators around the first lookout and three grounding wires running about 230 feet from the lookout to five-foot deep holes in the ground—all of this for lightning protection. At the Monumental Lookout he again installed insulators—seventy-three this time—and grounding wires which were 430 feet long. At both lookouts he also put in telephone wires. While he was working on these lookouts he discovered a fire north of one of them and he commented on the strong winds, which of course made the fires spread more rapidly. He also noted that when he arrived at the second lookout, the only shelter was a 7 ft x 9 ft tent that five men had to share! It must have been very cozy. In the later days of August and in early September he did similar work on at least five other fire lookouts in the area. Every time he returned "home" to Priest River, he would detail how much he spent for certain items: on September 25, 1925 it was "laundry-$.95, eats- $.25, shave and bath- $.50, photos- $2.10."

Dad also spent time in October 1925 on road work and bridge work in the Priest River region. He mentions tightening bolts on bridges, creosoting the timbers, putting white paint on handrails, and digging fire trenches around them. Many of his truck runs continue to mention hauling fire equipment. Because timber was the main industry, fires were the enemy, so Dad's work on the fire lookouts must have been considered of high importance. In his diary he also mentions making phone calls to Dunk; likely they were often in touch and saw each other as time permitted when Dad was in Priest River. By this time little Margaret would have been one and a half years old and walking. She was a gorgeous little child with her blond curly hair and a sweet smile as the photos show.

Dad seemed to have enjoyed his time working for the Great Northern Railroad in Vancouver and so in early 1926 he left Idaho for Seattle and an electrical engineering job with that railroad. He was part of the engineering team that electrified the famous Cascade Tunnel that went some eight miles through the Cascade Mountains below Stevens Pass in northern Washington. It was a gargantuan task, took some four years to complete, and was one of the longest railroad tunnels in the world at that time. The electrified tunnel opened to trains in January 1929. This project, which kept Dad very involved in all things railroad, was what most likely decided the future course of his career.

The year 1929 was a watershed year for both Dad and Dunk. Eileen and Dunk had been living in Priest River until 1928 but when Margaret was four they moved to Pierce, Idaho in the summers and to Orfino, Idaho in the winters. By late 1929 both Dunk and Eileen realized that for Margaret's education

Dunk and daughter Margaret, Missoula, 1930 (DY)

they would have to live in a larger city, so they moved back to Missoula, Montana for Margaret to start first grade there in 1930. They first lived in an apartment and then in a couple of rental houses until in 1937 they bought their house on East Beckwith Street, in a very desirable University of Montana neighborhood. Eileen had always been interested in a lifestyle that included the best social circles.

By now Eileen had become the first chief accountant for the USFS. Dunk at this time was working at the USFS Equipment

Dunk and Eileen by home in Missoula after pheasant hunt, c. 1940 (DY)

Development Shop in Missoula in charge of modifying existing equipment for USFS use. He was very mechanically oriented and much admired for the way he knew exactly how to make the necessary modifications to trucks, steam shovels, front-end loaders and other mechanized vehicles for optimal use in the virgin forests of the West. He travelled to various sites around the U.S. for the Forest Service to advise them on how to set up their shops. He and Eileen also often travelled to Washington, D.C. for USFS meetings. As a result they were away from home and separated from their only child much of the time. Margaret was brought up by a series of housekeepers. She rarely traveled with her parents and sometimes didn't see them for weeks at a time.

Dad, meanwhile, had decided to return East from whence he came. He had applied for and been offered a job as an electrical engineer with the Boston & Maine Railroad which he was to start in November 1929. He packed up his western life, and took leave of his friends in Seattle, Vancouver and Spokane. He then stopped by Missoula on his way east to bid farewell to Dunk, Eileen, and their now almost six-year old daughter Margaret. It must have been a difficult goodbye, as all of them knew that Boston and Missoula were thousands of miles apart.

Margaret Eileen Duncan York, age 90, at her farm near Missoula, Montana, 2014. (JBP)

# Chapter 8: The Missing Piece

Dad died in 1993 in his ninety-eighth year. It wasn't until after his death that I realized there was so much that I didn't know about his life. I was particularly interested then in finding out more about his World War I service, his relationship with Dunk, and his years in the West working and continuing his friendship with Dunk and his family. And so I started the search. Dad and Dunk had corresponded over the years, in particular always sending each other a Christmas card with news of their family. Dad had kept an address list on index cards of all of his old friends. So this was where I started in the early 2000s.

As a child, somehow, I knew that Dunk had died, because Dad would talk about Eileen and her second husband. And by the year 2000, Eileen born in 1898, would also have died. I knew from Dad's conversations that Dunk had a daughter quite a bit older than me, but I thought she might still be alive. And so I started to look for her—Dunk's daughter Margaret. After years of searching, and experiencing all the difficulties of trying to track down a woman whose name had changed in marriage, I finally came across a contact that seemed to be promising. It was for a "Margaret E. (perhaps for Eileen?) York" and was for a street address in western Montana. I sent this Margaret a letter with a copy of the photo of Dad and Dunk, asking her if she was the Margaret for whom I had been searching. Within ten days I received a letter in return acknowledging that, indeed, she was Dunk's daughter, now eighty-eight years old. She didn't have an email account, but she gave me her phone number. I immediately decided to call her.

The phone rang. I waited. It rang again. I waited. I had waited for years to find the person at the other end of the line. She was the closest link I had to my father's WWI years. Margaret was Dunk's daughter and only child—in a way, my contemporary, although significantly older. I was hoping that she could shed some light on our fathers' friendship, which had begun a hundred years before. It was a friendship that had lasted for several decades in the first half of the twentieth century. What could she tell me about her father and his life in his later years, and what, if anything, could she tell me about my father?

The phone rang again. Maybe she wasn't home, maybe she was ill, maybe she was just too old or too deaf to hear her phone. As she was several decades older than I was maybe she didn't like to speak on the phone. Maybe she didn't want to speak to me. Maybe …

Suddenly I heard a voice say, "Hello?"

I tried to compose myself, which wasn't easy; I had been looking forward to this day for many years. I was overcome with emotion to think that the person on the other end of the line, several thousand miles away in Western Montana, was really Dunk's daughter whom my father had spoken about with such affection. After a few seconds of awkward silence, I managed to utter, "Hello, is this Margaret?"

She answered with a rather isn't it obvious? "Yes, it is." And so began our connection to the events of a hundred years ago where our fathers had shared a friendship amid the death and destruction of "the war to end all wars."

After the phone conversation with Margaret, I kept asking myself the nagging question, "Why hadn't I taken the time to talk with my dad about all of this when I could have so easily done so?" This has, however, led me on a quest to learn more about the life and actors of World War I France and in the process connect Dad and Dunk to those far off times. After two research trips to the areas of France involved in WWI, following Dad's diary and photos from 1918-1919, and speaking to locals interested in and aware of the history of WWI France, I am just starting to understand better what Dad and Dunk must have experienced as two young men thrown into a war that very few people really wanted.

After Margaret and I spoke on the phone in December 2012, we stayed in touch by letter, which was her preferred method of communication. I learned that she had five children, four still living, with three daughters in Montana, and a son, Duncan, who lived on Cape Cod, in Massachusetts, not far from where I lived. Duncan, who was Dunk's grandson, was the keeper of all the family memorabilia having to do with WWI. In fact, Margaret had already sent him the photo of Dad and Dunk which I had sent to her in my first letter. He was eager to meet me and I was excited to meet him. During 2013 we met several times and exchanged stories about Dad and Dunk in WWI based on information I gleaned from my father's diary and photos, and that he took from Dunk's letters to Eileen, which he had in his possession. Then early in 2014, he called me one day to invite me to join him and his family on a trip to Montana to celebrate his mother's (Margaret's) ninetieth birthday. I was thrilled. I had been corresponding with Margaret and had been wanting to meet her for over a year, knowing that time was not on her side. This invitation gave me the impetus I needed, and I said that I would be absolutely delighted to accompany them and at long last meet Dunk's daughter.

On a late May day, after an early morning flight from Boston with a change in Minneapolis, we reached Missoula and drove directly to the farm where Margaret now lived, about forty-five minutes west of Missoula. I wasn't sure what to expect—I was going to be meeting a lady of ninety. Well, as it turned out, Margaret certainly didn't look or act like a ninety year old. We gave each other a big hug and then she said she had to feed the horses that were in the pasture next to her house. She proceeded to go out to the barn and heft part of a bale of hay onto her shoulders and carry it over to where the horses could eat it. I was amazed by her strength, vigor, and can-do attitude.

Margaret's and my first conversations were about family history. I learned that both of Dunk's parents were born in Scotland (Shetland Islands and Glasgow), but emigrated to U.S. in the 1880s. Dunk was born in Bismarck, North Dakota on route to Montana in 1888. Two younger sisters were born in Montana in the 1890s. The family originally owned a homestead lot (160 acres) up in the Rattlesnake Creek area slightly

Margaret with hay to feed horses, 2014. (JPB)

northeast of downtown Missoula where they had a farm. Dunk's parents believed in the importance of education and so donated some of their land for a school on Rattlesnake Creek for local children. When the Montana Power Company took over the Rattlesnake Creek drainage area by eminent domain in the early 1900s, their land was taken and their house was burned to make way for the power project. The Duncan family then went down to live in Missoula. Dunk most likely went to elementary school in Rattlesnake Creek and then went to Roosevelt High School in Missoula starting about 1902. It is not clear, however, whether he left to go to work for the U.S. Forest Service before he graduated. As his letters to Eileen indicate, he wrote quite well with good vocabulary, but often misspelled words.

What did Margaret remember about her father? When I asked her this question, she indicated that they didn't really have a very close relationship and that she was somewhat afraid of him. She commented that he was "older" when she was born and maybe not used to children. He was away a lot for his Forest Service work and Margaret said that she was really brought up by housekeepers until she married at age twenty-one. She also recalled that Dunk always had a car, and as his letters to Eileen also indicated, one of their favorite Sunday pastimes was taking a spin in the car out in the countryside.

According to Margaret, her mother Eileen was a social climber and cared a lot about her appearance. She and Dunk took many trips without Margaret. They often travelled around the West to other U.S. Forest Service locations for work, as well as to Washington, D.C. for annual USFS meetings. Dunk never talked to Margaret about the war, she remarked, but she said, "Doug Burckett was a household name. They talked about him often." So neither Margaret nor I had had any lengthy discussions about World War I with our fathers.

I had always had a very close, loving relationship with my father, so after this conversation with Margaret, I was stunned. How could Dunk not have cared to spend more time with his

Margaret and son Duncan look over old family photos, 2014. (JBP)

only child, to have shown her the West that he loved, to have taught her to ride and hunt? How could he and Eileen have left her to be brought up by a series of housekeepers? Of course times were different and life was often more difficult almost one hundred years ago; so there may have been good reasons for Dunk and Eileen's parental decisions. These questions still haunt me. And I was disappointed that Margaret was unable to tell me much at all about her father or about his relationship with my father. But then, of course, Margaret was only twenty-one when Dunk had died of appendicitis in 1945, and that was seventy years ago.

The two daughters meet—Jenifer and Margaret, Montana, 2014. (JBP)

Dugout at Verrières Farm where Dad lived for a month in the fall of 1918 during the Meuse-Argonne Offensive. Photo taken June 2017. (JBP)

# Chapter 9:
# "Over There" a Century Later

Before connecting with Margaret in 2012 I had already taken one trip back to France in 2011 to the Verdun area to follow my father's footsteps in order to try to better understand what he had experienced nearly a century before. I had used his diary entries and photos to follow his trail and managed to take many photos from the same vantage points from which he had taken photos so many years before. I had spoken to locals whose parents or grandparents had been there during World War I, I had gone to museums and historical sites, and I had visited the incredibly moving American Cemetery north of Verdun near Montfaucon in Romagne. I had gone inside the forts of Douaumont and Vaux, just east of Verdun—front-line forts that had played a key role in the war.

In one small village the mayor's husband had taken me to a fort in the forest above the town where he had played as a child over sixty years before. By then the structure was almost totally covered by bushes, trees, and brambles. It had taken us an hour to find it going back and forth on the many small trails in the woods—paths that he hadn't been on for some fifty years.

I had visited the Verdun Memorial, Battlefields, and Ossuary which were a sobering reminder of the horrors and millions of deaths that occurred in World War I. I even managed to find the former Miribel Barracks on east side of the Meuse River in Verdun where Dad and Dunk had been billeted in the spring of 1919 before returning home. It still belonged to the French Ministry of Defense, but was obviously no longer in use as the entry gate was rusting and padlocked. I had driven down the "Voie Sacrée"—the Sacred Route—the road leading from Verdun to Bar-le-Duc which was the only road in and out of Verdun during the dreadful ten-month assault on that city in 1916. It had experienced truck and wagon traffic twenty-four hours a day seven days a week during that turbulent period

One of the many piers at Brest in 2017, where American transports had tied up in 1918. (JBP)

in order to supply the French forces in Verdun with what was needed to continue the defense of the city.

But what I hadn't had in 2011 was much detailed information about what Dad and Dunk were actually doing at the time. After making contact with Margaret in 2012 and meeting Duncan in 2013 and then Margaret in 2014, I was privileged to be granted access to all of Dunk's letters to Eileen. Many of these letters, as we have seen in previous chapters, provided great detail of what the engineers of Wagon Company #3 were doing and how they were feeling. This was the absolutely necessary complement to the detailed, but brief, diary entries made by Dad and to his carefully labeled photos.

So, armed with Dunk's letters, Dad's diary and photos, and several articles about the Engineer Regiments in WWI that I had found published by the U.S. Army Corps of Engineers

The author meets photographer Monique Thuriot-Prémery, daughter of photographer Pierre Prémery, who had probably taken Dad and Dunk's photo in his Nevers studio in 1918. (JBP)

Publications Depot, I knew I had to return once again to the World War I region of France. And so it was that in June 2017 I planned my trek, this time encompassing the three areas that Dad and Dunk had spent time in during their fifteen months in France—Brest, Nevers, and Verdun.

The highpoints of my trip were numerous and varied, but aside from the many, many very welcoming and extremely helpful French people that I met, and the historical sites and museums that I visited, two experiences stand out above all others. First was learning about the presence of and construction for the Nevers Cut-Off. Few Americans today have ever heard of the Nevers Cut-Off although it was the most important railroad construction project in WWI France. And few French, including those now living in the Nevers region, have heard of it. Memory fades over a hundred years and as the generations pass. It is mostly the grandchildren, great grandchildren and great-great grandchildren now who inhabit the land south of Nevers where the cut-off passed through. I was able to link up with a local historian from Sermoise, on the eastern end of the cut-off, who drove me along country lanes parallel to and crisscrossing the former railroad. He guided me through brambles to the edge of the Loire River to show me the still-extant wooden pilings protruding above water level that had supported the railroad bridge.

It was due to a felicitous set of circumstances that I met my Nevers Cut-Off guide. It all started with a WWI aficionado's website which put me in contact with the daughter, Lucy, of a French WWI war bride from the Nevers area. After emailing Lucy and finding that we lived less than two hours away from each other, I paid her a visit one Saturday morning in late April 2017 to exchange WWI stories. Thinking that I would probably stay for an hour or two at most, I was amazed that after five hours we both realized we were hungry and then shocked at how many hours had passed. After being served a delicious lunch with French bread, made by Lucy from her French mother's recipe, we continued to go over more WWI documents. Lucy had just published a book, based on her French mother's stories, about growing up in a small village south of Nevers. Her father, an American army medic, had worked at the nearby American hospital in Mars-sur-Allier, where Lucy's mother had been his French tutor. Lucy's close connection with this village, Moiry, and the neighboring town of Saint Parize-le-Châtel had been going on for several decades and she was a frequent visitor there and supporter of the town's school and historical connection to WWI. In fact, she was going to be there in June to celebrate the dedication of the WWI American-built hospital water tower—the only part of the hospital complex still standing—to commemorate the American's support to France in WWI. When she found out that I, too, was going to be in Nevers at the same time, she invited me to join her in the celebrations and gave me a list of her contacts who might be able to help me with discovering my Dad's reason for being in the Nevers area.

And so the email traffic started, first with a Lieutenant Colonel Durand, who was part of a committee which was organizing a project about the history of the American Expeditionary Forces (AEF) in Nevers to present to the public in 2017. Then communication began with Gianni, an avid amateur historian from St. Parize-le-Châtel, who was gathering material on the Mars-sur-Allier Hospital in order to create a guided tour of its former grounds, complete with twenty-four informational plaques, each sporting a small flag pole with an American flag. LTC Durand and I started exchanging information. He was interested in my father's diary and so I sent him the parts which referred to Dad's time in Nevers, which he promptly translated into French so they could be used as part of the AEF history project. When he found out that Dad had been with an Engineer Regiment he asked me if I knew about the Nevers Cut-Off. I told him that I had never heard of it and so he then sent me pages of information (in French), along with maps and drawings describing the planning and execution of this most important American rail project in WWI France. I then reread Dunk's letters and Dad's diary and voila! There it was in Dunk's letters describing the work on the project, with hundreds of men. Also, it was in Dad's diary entries recording their camp at Sermoise, one of the villages on the route, and a later diary entry noted how they had returned from the Front via the "Never Cut-Off, which had been constructed by the 23rd engineers." Right then and there, I was hooked. I knew I had to go to see the remains of the Nevers Cut-Off with my very own eyes.

Enter Jean-François, a historian from Sermoise, on the route of the cut-off just south of Nevers. The colonel had arranged for him to be my guide for that June afternoon the day after I arrived in Nevers. As Jean-François drove me around the country roads that mostly paralleled, but in some cases actually crossed over, the route of the cut-off, I was amazed to still be able to very clearly distinguish the raised rail bed that had been constructed a hundred years ago. The rails had been removed and sold in the 1920s after the French government declared that after the war, with no longer any need for this rail line, the land

Jean-François, my guide to the Nevers Cut-Off at Sermoise, 2017. (JBP)

The Cut-Off road bed was still visible in 2017. (JBP)

The Cut-Off bridge pilings in the Loire River as they looked in 2017. (PAN)

should be returned to its former use. The rail bed, however, in some cases was still used as a farm track. But the most thrilling part of this walk back in history was when we left the car and walked several hundred yards through tall grass and prickly bushes to the edge of the Loire River. There was no longer any railroad bridge across the river, but just protruding above the water level we could clearly view the original bridge pilings, made of trees pounded into the river bed to hold up the railway bridge across the Loire. They had been sawed off in the 1920s to about water level, so as not to disturb the flow of the river, but they were still there after a hundred years. It was a truly amazing sight.

    The second highpoint during my June 2017 trip was finding and standing inside the dugout at Verrières Farm in the Argonne Forest where Dad had lived at the time of the Armistice. Finding the "dugout attached to the office" in a "camp in Hesse Forest near Dombasle" in a "good location only quite muddy," as Dad had written in his diary for October 18, 1918, was a challenge.

On my 2011 research trip to the Verdun area I had tried to visit many of the locations mentioned by Dad in his diary or which appeared in his carefully labelled photographs. Thanks to a reproduction of a 1916 map of the Verdun area, I was able to locate a "Verrières-en-Hesse" in the middle of the Hesse Forest, a section of the larger Argonne Forest, about three miles north of Dombasle. It was a late afternoon, after a full day of visiting other sites photographed by Dad, when I set out on the main road from Verdun to Dombasle to try to find the right dirt road that would lead me to the Verrières Farm. After passing the village of Dombasle, I reached the hamlet of Récicourt where I encountered a narrow tarred road going north into the Hesse Forest, which very soon became a dirt track. I followed this dirt track about two miles until coming to a T junction. There I turned right and within a mile saw fields of wheat and in the distance a building. It was in the correct location map-wise to be Verrières Farm. As I arrived at the entrance to the farmyard, two huge, fierce-looking Alsatian dogs came running out to my car. I was so tired after my full day of going from place to place that I wasn't ready to deal with these unfriendly canines and so I turned the car around, after taking a few photos, and returned to Verdun.

In June 2017 I was determined to make the trek again to Verrières Farm and this time I promised myself that I would deal with whatever eventualities presented themselves. Again I set off from Verdun, passed through Dombasle, and then managed to find the narrow road, still mostly dirt, that left from Récicourt. The journey seemed mildly familiar and I noted that the quality of the road had definitely improved—no more deep ruts or large depressions—had the 23rd Engineers been there? As the wheat fields came into view I saw that sprinkled among the wheat were scores of red poppies. It was a glorious day and the poppies seemed to be a good omen, a sign that a WWI encounter might be in my near future.

The approach to Verrières Farm, 2017. (JBP)

Then the farm buildings appeared on the far side of the wheat fields. As I approached the entrance to the farm, I waited with bated breath for the arrival of the barking dogs, but no dogs appeared, to my great relief. To my even greater relief a man came out into the farmyard. I stopped the car, got out, and wished him a "bonjour." He was wearing a white shirt, black pants and a long brown leather apron, which gave the impression that he was some kind of a tradesman. His face looked as if he were in his late forties. We introduced ourselves and he told me that his name was Ludovic and that he was a farrier, one of five in the Meuse region. He had bought Verrières Farm from its previous owner about ten years before. He noted that the farm had been built in 1740 and showed me the date carved in a stone lintel over one of the gates. The farm, he commented, had originally belonged to the monks of Verdun who used it to grow food for the clergy of Verdun. He also recounted that there had been a munitions depot near the farm. Early on in the war the Germans had blown it up and partially destroyed the farm.

Ludovic at the entrance to Verrières Farm. (JBP)

Then it was my turn to talk and explain why I was there. I told Ludovic that my father had been camped at the farm during WWI, for about four weeks from just before to just after the Armistice. I told him I was interested in seeing this spot where my father had lived some hundred years ago. As Ludovic showed me around the farm buildings, he said that Dad would not have been at the farm, but rather at an 'abri'—a dugout shelter—in the forest just north of the farm. I then asked him if he could take me to the dugout, but he replied that his friend knew much more about it and would be the best person to take me there, perhaps on another day. As I didn't have another day, I asked Ludovic to point me in the right direction, but feeling my sense of urgency, he then agreed to show me the dugout himself.

As we walked down the dirt road toward the forest, a faint glint of rusty metal in the road caught my eye. As I leaned down to pick it up, I realized that it was not just any old piece of metal, and as Ludovic immediately confirmed, it was a

Ludovic about to lead author to dugout in the woods behind them. (JBP)

fragment—a piece of shrapnel—from a WWI shell. He said that every square meter of this area was filled with the remains of shells and grenades. He, himself, had an extensive collection of this war materiel which he later showed me before we left the farm.

We soon left the dirt road and entered a makeshift path at the edge of a wheat field which led to a wooded area. As Ludovic hadn't been to the dugout recently, it took us a bit of wandering through brush and bushes, up and over a hillock, until we finally found its entrance by sliding down a dirt slope holding on to some thick vines. And there it was. I could barely believe that we had found it, found the place where Dad had lived and worked from October 18, 1918 ("On October 18 moved again from near Esnes to camp in Hesse Forest near Dombasle. Jackson and I have dugout attached to office. Good location only quite muddy. Have a horse of my own now and have to curry it every A.M. and have to feed it.") until November 16, 1918 ("Nov. 16. Sat. Broke camp at Verriere Farm north Dombasle this A.M. and moved to second farm in bowl of land north of Doulcon on Meuse opposite Dun… Camp is in farm buildings which are shot up by Amer. Artillery …").

The Verrières Farm dugout would have been just a couple of miles south of the German lines when the Meuse-Argonne Offensive started on September 26, 1918. When Dad was living there from mid October to mid November it would have been about six miles from the Front, or more as the Front moved north when the Americans and French drove the Germans further back. Dad would have heard the daily exchange of fire, the artillery barrages, and have seen the airplanes and dirigibles used in reconnaissance operations.

The dugout was almost completely covered with trees, undergrowth and what you might call a carpet of ivy. The entrance was composed of a doorway, now without a door, about three feet wide and five feet tall. To the right of the door and about midway up the wall was a two foot by eighteen inch window opening, also now without the actual pane. On the wall to the left of the door at about the level of the top of the aforementioned window was a circular opening about five inches in diameter surrounded by metal. This was where the stove pipe would have exited the dugout. Above the structure, in the middle of the field of ivy, was a hole, which would have probably had a small pipe extruding from it to provide for ventilation.

The building itself was made of a huge curved piece of corrugated metal, such as you see used today for some airplane hangars. The front outside walls to the right and left of the entry door were made of wood with a coating of cement, now partially degraded after one hundred years. As we entered the dark interior we saw that the structure consisted of two large rooms, the "dugout attached to office" of Dad's diary description. Each room was some nine feet wide at ground level and easily seven feet high at the highest point, so that there was no problem standing up straight while inside the structure. It actually felt quite roomy. There was a now nearly-destroyed wooden wall and door between the two rooms. On the inside of

Close-up of dugout's front entrance with stovepipe hole on left. (JBP)

Inside the two-room dugout looking toward the office area. (JBP)

the dugout to the left were some strong wooden beams coming out horizontally from the wall in three ascending rows with two beams per row with about two feet between each row. This was undoubtedly the location of the basic bunks where Dad and his fellow soldiers slept. The floor was dirt. It was littered with rocks, bits of cement and many, many wooden timbers coming from the former wooden wall sections. The wall at the far end of the structure was almost totally demolished and so let in a lot of light. Despite its current state of disrepair, the dugout was still there a hundred years later. I was moved with a feeling, almost of reverence, for a humble abode which had sheltered my father one hundred years ago.

How had Dad felt about this fairly primitive living quarters, I wondered? Had it been a step up from the previous camp near Esnes? Had he been able to gather enough wood to keep a fire burning in the little cast iron stove in order to keep warm during the chilly autumn days in November? Had he been able to use it to cook warm meals? And had anybody been living in the actual Verrières farmhouse or had the owners, who fled before the Germans arrived, locked it up and left it uninhabited? What exactly had Dad and his buddy Jackson been doing here? We know they had an office and had to get reports out? Were these military reports of troops movements or were they concerned with materials and supplies used or needed? Did Dad have a radio or was all communication face-to-face or by written notes? We know Dad had a horse, but probably no motorized transport, as given the condition of the farm roads today, it would be unlikely that they were passable for trucks or cars in 1918.

Where was Dunk and where were the rest of Wagon Company #3? We know that Dad and Dunk met up again on November 16th, the day Dad left the dugout and moved to the badly damaged farm buildings near Doulcon on the Meuse River. And from then on they were together all the way back to the U.S. But why was Dad seemingly separated from most of the others in his company while living in the dugout?

We will never know the answers to these questions. But we do now know better the story of a WWI friendship, the bond between two young soldier-engineers who met and became close buddies during the death and destruction of the Great War. It is the story of a friendship which blossomed during tough times in a foreign land, where trust and caring counted. It is the story of a friendship which has endured throughout a century and continues now into the fourth generation of Dad and Dunk's progeny.

Douglas Burckett (Dad) and his wife Phillippa Burckett with their youngest granddaughter on a hike in New Hampshire in 1992. (JBP)

# Epilogue

George W. Duncan "Dunk" continued working with the U.S. Forest Service in Missoula, Montana until he died of a ruptured appendix in 1945 at age fifty-seven.

Eileen Duncan (Dunk's wife) remarried in 1965, twenty years after Dunk had died. She and her second husband lived in Missoula, in the home she and Dunk had bought, until she died in 1985 at age eighty-seven.

Margaret, Dunk's daughter, died in May 2016 at the age of ninety-two, still living independently in her farmhouse in Western Montana. Her three surviving daughters all live within a mile of her farm. Most of her thirteen grandchildren and some dozen great-grandchildren live in the state of Montana, most in the Missoula area. Her son Duncan and his family live on Cape Cod in Massachusetts.

Douglas M. Burckett (Dad) married Phillippa Patey in 1941 in the Boston area. They had met eight years earlier on an Appalachian Mountain Club (A.M.C.) ski trip in the Laurentian Mountains in Canada. He and Phillippa lived in Cambridge with their two children until the mid 1950s, at which time they built a house in a suburb just west of Boston. After having to retire at age sixty-five from the Boston & Maine Railroad, Dad worked another thirty-two years as the Chairman of the Assessors of his town. He and Phillippa were both very active in the A.M.C. and in various ski and conservation organizations — hiking, skiing, and travelling into their eighties and nineties. Both of them died in the mid 1990s of natural causes.

Fort Slocum, New York, where Dad enlisted, was a military post from 1867 on David's Island off the coast of New Rochelle, New York. Used as a recruit depot in WWI, it was closed and abandoned in 1965.

Camp Meade, Maryland, about twenty miles southwest of Baltimore, was one of sixteen cantonments authorized by the U.S. government in 1917 to be constructed for Army training units for WWI. From 1917-1918 two thousand buildings were constructed and 103,000 men were trained there for overseas duty (Dad and Dunk from December 1917 to January 1918). It was also used as a training center in the early months of World War II. Now called Fort George Meade, it is a U.S. Army installation under the Department of Defense and home of the Defense Information School, the Defense Media Activity, the National Security Agency, the Defense Information Systems Agency, and headquarters of the U.S. Cyber Command.

Camp Laurel, not far from Camp Meade, in Laurel, Maryland, was the Maryland State Fairground when it was taken over as an Army camp to handle the overflow from Camp Meade in WWI. Laurel's closed cotton mill was also used as a barracks and a site for dances at that time. Thousands of soldiers, mainly engineers from the 23rd (Dad and Dunk's regiment), 66th and 50th Regiments passed through Camp Laurel. It has now reverted back to its original use as the Laurel Park Racetrack.

Camp Glen Burnie, close to Camp Meade, was only a temporary camp to accommodate the huge numbers of soldiers enlisting and being drafted for WWI. It was a tent camp on the former Naval Rifle Range and was decommissioned after the Armistice in 1918.

Camp Upton on Long Island, New York, where Dad and Dunk's Wagon Company #3 passed out of service in June 1919, was used as a Japanese internment camp during World War II. It later became Brookhaven National Laboratories.

# Selected Bibliography

Barlow, Aaron. 2017. *Doughboys on the Western Front: Memories of American Soldiers in the Great War*. Santa Barbara, CA: Praeger.

Barthas, Louis. 2014. *Poilu: The World War I Notebooks of Corporal Louis Barthas, Barrelmaker, 1914-1918*. New Haven, CT: Yale University Press.

Baxter, John. 2014. *Paris at the End of the World: The City of Light during the Great War, 1914-1918*. New York: Harper Perennial.

Berg, A. Scott. 2013. *Wilson*. New York: Putnam.

Boyd, Thomas. 2008. *Through the Wheat: A Novel of the World War I Marines*. Lincoln, NE: University of Nebraska Press.

Bull, Stephen. 2014. *The Old Front Line: The Centenary of the Western Front in Pictures*. Havertown, PA: Casemate Publishers.

Bull, Stephen. 2010. *Trench: A History of Trench Warfare on the Western Front*. Oxford: Osprey Publishing.

Camp, Richard D. 2008. *The Devil Dogs at Belleau Wood: U.S. Marines in World War I*. St. Paul, MN: MBI.

Carruthers, Bob. 2014. *Private Hitler's War, 1914-1918*. Barnsley, UK: Pen and Sword Books.

Carter, Miranda. 2010. *The Three Emperors: Three Cousins, Three Empires and the Road to World War One*. London: Fig Tree.

Castle, Ian. 2015. The *First Blitz: Bombing London in the First World War*. Oxford: Osprey Publishing.

Clark, Christopher M. 2013. *The Sleepwalkers: How Europe Went to War in 1914*. New York: Harper.

Clarke, P. F. 2017. *The Locomotive of War: Money, Empire, Power and Guilt*. UK: Bloomsbury Publishing.

Connelly, Charlie. 2014. *The Forgotten Soldier: He Went off to Fight in the Great War - and Never Came Home*. London: Harper Element.

Coativy, Yves (Ed.).2017. *Cahiers de l'Iroise*. No. 225. Brest, France: Société d'Études de Brest et du Léon.

Dalessandro, Robert J. 2016. *Over There: America in the Great War*. Mechanicsburg, PA: Stackpole Publishing.

Desbarats, M. and J.F. Jondeau. 2017. *La Présence Américaine dans la Nièvre*. Sermoise, France: La Sermoisienne.

Downing, Taylor. 2016. *Secret Warriors: The Spies, Scientists and Code Breakers of World War I*. New York: Pegasus Books.

Ebel, Jonathan H. 2010. *Faith in the Fight: Religion and the American Soldier in the Great War*. Princeton, NJ: Princeton University Press.

Emmerson, Charles. c2013. *1913: In Search of the World before the Great War*. New York: Public Affairs.

Englund, Peter. 2011. *The Beauty and the Sorrow: An Intimate History of the First World War*. New York: Alfred A. Knopf.

Englund, Will. 2017. *March 1917: On the Brink of War and Revolution*. New York: W.W. Norton and Company.

Fawaz, Leila Tarazi. 2014. *A Land of Aching Hearts: The Middle East in the Great War*. Cambridge, Massachusetts: Harvard University Press.

Finnegan, Terrence J. 2015. *"A Delicate Affair" on the Western Front: America Learns How to Fight a Modern War in the Wöevre Trenches*. Gloucestershire, UK: History Press Limited.

Forty, Simon. 2013. *Mapping the First World War: Battlefields of the Great Conflict from above*. London: Conway.

Fussell, Paul. 2013. *The Great War and Modern Memory*. New York, NY: Oxford University Press, USA.

Grant, R.G. 2014. *World War I: The Definitive Visual History: From Sarajevo to Versailles*. London: D K Publishing.

Harris, Stephen L. 2008. *Duffy's War: Fr. Francis Duffy, Wild Bill Donovan, and the Irish Fighting 69th in World War I*. Washington, DC: Potomac Books.

Hastings, Max. 2013. *Catastrophe 1914: Europe Goes to War*. Oregon: Blackstone.

Hendricks, Charles.1993. *Combat and Construction: U.S. Army Engineers in World War I*. Fort Belvoir, Virginia: Office of History, U.S. Army Corps of Engineers.

Herwig, Holger H. c2009. *The Marne, 1914: The Opening of World War I and the Battle That Changed the World*. New York: Random House.

Higonnet, Margaret R. 1999. *Lines of Fire: Women Writers of World War I*. New York: Plume.

Hill, Duncan. 2013. *The Great War: A Pictorial History*. London: Atlantic Publishing.

Hillier, Stephanie. 2014. *Long Way to Tipperary: Bombs, Bullets and Bravery in the Trenches of WWI, The Diary of Maurice Graffet Neal*. Cirencester,UK: Memoirs Publishing.

Hochschild, Adam. 2011. *To End All Wars: A Story of Loyalty and Rebellion, 1914-1918*. Boston: Houghton Mifflin Harcourt.

Jeffery, Keith. 2016. *1916: A Global History*. UK: Bloomsbury.

Junger, Ernst. 1929. *The Storm of Steel*. London: Penguin Books.

Keegan, John. 2000. *The First World War*. Norwalk, CT: Easton Press.

Kessler, Harry. 2011. *Journey to the Abyss: The Diaries of Count Harry Kessler, 1880-1918*. New York: Alfred A. Knopf.

Lacey, Jim. 2010. *Pershing: A Biography*. New York: Macmillan.

Landau, Henry. 1938. *Spreading the Spy Net. The Story of a British Spy Director. [With Plates, Including a Portrait.]*. London: Jarrolds.

Landau, Henry. 2016. *Spy Net: The Man Who Ran the White Lady, the Greatest Intelligence Operation of the First World War*. London: Biteback Publishing.

Lang, Sean. 2014. *First World War for Dummies*. London: IWM.

Larson, Erik. 2017. *Dead Wake: The Last Crossing of the Lusitania*. New York: Crown Publishing Group.

Laskin, David. 2010. *The Long Way Home: An American Journey from Ellis Island to the Great War*. 1st ed. New York: Harper.

Mackin, Elton E. 1996. *Suddenly We Didn't Want to Die: Memoirs of a World War I Marine*. New York: Penguin Random House.

MacMillan, Margaret. 2014. *The War That Ended Peace: How Europe Abandoned Peace for the First World War*. New York: Random House.

McCarter, Jeremy. 2017. *Bright as Fire: Young Radicals and the Life and Death of American Ideals, 1912-1920*. [Place of publication not identified]: Random House.

McMeekin, Sean. 2013a. *July 1914: Countdown to War*. New York: Basic Books.

McMeekin, Sean. 2013b. *The Russian Origins of the First World War*. Cambridge, MA: Belknap Press of Harvard University Press.

Meyer, G. J. 2006. *A World Undone: The Story of the Great War, 1914-1918*. New York: Delacorte Press.

Mosier, John. 2014. *The Myth of the Great War: A New Military History of World War 1*. New York: HarperCollins.

Neiberg, Michael S. 2011. *Dance of the Furies: Europe and the Outbreak of World War I*. Cambridge, MA: Belknap Press of Harvard University Press.

Nelson, James Carl. 2010. *The Remains of Company D*. New York: St. Martin's Press.

Noppen, Ryan. 2015a. *German Commerce Raiders 1914-18*. Oxford, UK: Osprey Publishing.

Noppen, Ryan. 2015b. *Ottoman Navy Warships 1914-18*. Oxford, UK: Osprey Publishing.

Osborn, Patrick and Marc Romanych. 2016. *The Hindenburg Line*. Oxford, UK: Osprey Publishing.

Pardoe, Blaine. 2008. *Terror of the Autumn Skies: The True Story of Frank Luke, America's Rogue Ace of World War I*. New York: Skyhorse Publishing, Inc.

Persico, Joseph E. 2005. *11th Month, 11th Day, 11th Hour: Armistice Day, 1918, World War I and Its Violent Climax*. London: Arrow Books.

Pickthall, Barry. 2016. *The Red Baron: Rare Photographs from Wartime Archives*. Barnsley, Yorkshire, UK: Pen & Sword Books.

Reynolds, David. 2014. *The Long Shadow: The Legacies of the Great War in the Twentieth Century*. New York: W.W. Norton & Co.

Rogan, Eugene L. 2015. *The Fall of the Ottomans: The Great War in the Middle East*. New York: Hachette Book Group.

Romanych, M. 2014. *42cm "Big Bertha" and German Siege Artillery of World War I*. Oxford: Osprey Publishing.

Ross, John F. 2015. *Enduring Courage: Ace Pilot Eddie Rickenbacker and the Dawn of the Age of Speed*. New York: MacMillan.

Rubin, Richard. 2013. *The Last of the Doughboys: The Forgotten Generation and Their Forgotten World War*. Boston: Houghton Miflin-Mariner.

Rubin, Richard. 2017. *Back Over There*. New York: St. Martin's Press.

Sáenz, José de la Luz. (Ed. And Trans. by Emilio Zamora) 2014. *The World War I Diary of José de La Luz Sáenz*. College Station, TX: Texas A&M University. Original Spanish version published in 1933 by Artes Gráficas, San Antonio, TX.

Safran, Gabriella. 2010. *Wandering Soul: The Dybbuk's Creator, S. An-Sky*. Cambridge, MA: Belknap Press of Harvard University Press.

Shaara, Jeff. 2004. *To the Last Man: A Novel of the First World War*. New York: Ballantine Books.

Sheffield, G. D. 2014. *A Short History of the First World War*. London: One World Publisher.

Sims, William Sowden. 1920. *The Victory at Sea*. London: John Murray.

Stevenson, D. 2011. *With Our Backs to the Wall: Victory and Defeat in 1918*. Cambridge, MA: Belknap Press of Harvard University Press.

Strachan, Hew. 2014. *The Oxford Illustrated History of the First World War.* Oxford: OUP.

Taylor, Col. 1919. *Historical Report of the Chief Engineer, Including All Operations of the Engineer Department, AEF, 1917-1919.* Washington, DC: Government Printing Office.

Taylor, Edmond. 1989. *The Fall of the Dynasties: The Collapse of the Old Order 1905-1922.* New York: Dorset Press.

Taylor, Peter. 2015. *Weird War One: Intriguing Items and Fascinating Feats from the First World War.* Chicago: University of Chicago Press.

Tuchman, Barbara W. 1962. *The Guns of August.* New York: Macmillan.

Williamson, Walter. (Ed. by Doreen Priddey) 2013. *A Tommy at Ypres: Walter's War.* Stroud, England: Amberley Publishing.

Woolley, Charles. 2004. *Echoes of Eagles: A Son's Search for His Father and the Legacy of America's First Fighter Pilots.* New York: NAL Caliber.

# Acknowledgements

I would like to thank the dozens of French men and women with whom I met and spoke about World War I during my research trips in 2011 and 2017, many of whom were parts of larger groups and so remain nameless. In particular, however, I would like to thank my hosts and guides in Brest, Nevers and Verdun. In Brest, Yves Coativy, President of the local historical society (Société d'Études de Brest et du Léon), took time out of his very busy schedule to guide me around the most important sites in Brest having to do with World War I. This included the well-developed port area as well as the site of the Pontanezen Barracks, now abandoned land with no remaining buildings from WWI times, but with a few roads laid out in a current scheme to develop the area for residential and business use.

In the Nevers region, my deepest appreciation goes to Lt. Colonel Pierre-Eric Durand for sharing with me his knowledge of the American presence in WWI Nevers and for arranging my visits to various sites and with various individuals in the area; to Jean-François Jondeau, historian and expert in the role of American engineers in building the Nevers (railway) Cut-Off and my guide to viewing the remains of the cut-off road bed and bridge pilings in the Loire River; to Gianni Belli, American WWI history buff and driving force behind the Mars-sur-Allier American WWI Army Hospital historical tour, who personally showed me the twenty-four sites he had meticulously set up with informational posters sporting American flags; to Elisabeth Franc, Director of the Marzy Museum, and her team who organized a riveting exhibition on the American Expeditionary Forces in Nevers in WWI, which included many original WWI photos taken by the renowned Nevers photographer Pierre Prémery and donated by his daughter, Monique Thuriot-Prémery who still carries on her father's trade; and to Colette Mayot, Director of Hérédit, a historical society in St. Parize-le-Châtel, who shared with me many interesting WWI historical documents. In Verdun, my sincere thanks go to Jean Marie, President of his local chapter of Souvenir Français, for being my guide in the Dun-sur-Meuse area and for giving me a private tour of the WWI history museum which he founded in order to keep alive the memory of the role American forces played in the Meuse area in WWI; to Jean Dobin for showing me the hidden remains of the WWI fort at Moulainville and for relating anecdotes of WWI in that area; to Ludovic Nieder for telling me about the history of Verrières Farm and then leading me to the WWI dugout where my father had lived in November 1918; to Natacha Glaudel, acquisitions director at the Memorial de Verdun, for sharing WWI materials with me; to Lionel Frémont, Verdun historian and preservationist, who spent time with me and shared documents concerning WWI.

In the U.S. I struck a gold mine when I made contact with Lucy DeVries Duffy from Cape Cod, whose French mother lived in the Nevers area and whose American father worked at the Mars-sur-Allier Hospital. Lucy put me in touch with virtually all of my contacts in Nevers for which I am eternally grateful to her. Many thanks, also, to Brigadier General (ret.) and military historian Leonid Kondratiuk, who pointed me in the right direction to access Army engineering documents.

To Duncan York, George "Dunk" Duncan's grandson and keeper of his grandfather's WWI memorabilia, I owe a huge debt for allowing me to use the letters that Dunk wrote to his girlfriend (later wife), Eileen, in this book. He also shared family anecdotes with me and then invited me to accompany him to Montana to help celebrate his mother Margaret's ninetieth birthday. To her, Dunk's daughter, I owe a special thanks for sharing her family stories and photographs with me. My sincere appreciation for reviewing the manuscript, and offering their advice on how it could be improved, goes to Dennis, Duncan, Laura, Sully, Susan, and Walter. My even greater appreciation goes to Ron for helping to put it all together.

Finally, to the two men who were the raison d'être for this book and who made the detail in this book possible – Dad and Dunk – a million thanks to Dunk for writing such tender and also culturally-illuminating letters, often under less than ideal conditions, and to Dad for keeping such an accurate diary and for so faithfully labelling his photos.

# About the Author

Jenifer Burckett-Picker has served for the past fifteen years as the Director of the PhD Program at the Fletcher School of Law & Diplomacy at Tufts University. Before that she worked for international development agencies in Latin America, and was an assistant professor of Spanish at Simmons College in Boston. She is a passionate history buff, and has written books and articles on subjects ranging from the history of seven generations of a Baja California (Mexico) family to Guarani creation myths from the jungles of Paraguay. An inveterate traveler, fluent in several languages, she has cherished every minute of her trips to World War I France to discover her father's journey "over there" from the perspective of a century on. She lives in the Boston area with her family.

180509

www.ingramcontent.com/pod-product-compliance
Lightning Source LLC
Chambersburg PA
CBHW070551010526
44118CB00012B/1291